THE ATTACK ON PEARL HARBOR

MILESTONES
IN
AMERICAN HISTORY

MILESTONES
IN
AMERICAN HISTORY

THE ATTACK ON PEARL HARBOR

THE UNITED STATES ENTERS WORLD WAR II

JOHN C. DAVENPORT

CHELSEA HOUSE
PUBLISHERS
An imprint of Infobase Publishing

The Attack on Pearl Harbor

Chelsea House
An imprint of Infobase Publishing
132 West 31st Street
New York, NY 10001

Library of Congress Cataloging-in-Publication Data

Davenport, John, 1960–
  The attack on Pearl Harbor : the United States enters World War II / John C. Davenport.
  p. cm. — (Milestones in American history)
  Includes bibliographical references and index.
  ISBN 978-1-60413-010-2 (hbk.)
  1. Pearl Harbor (Hawaii), Attack on, 1941—Juvenile literature. I. Title. II. Series.
  D767.92.D37 2008
  940.54'26693—dc22   2008019294

Chelsea House books are available at special discounts when purchased in bulk quantities for businesses, associations, institutions, or sales promotions. Please call our Special Sales Department in New York at (212) 967-8800 or (800) 322-8755.

You can find Chelsea House on the World Wide Web at http://www.chelseahouse.com

Text design by Erik Lindstrom
Cover design by Ben Peterson

Printed in the United States of America

Bang NMSG 10 9 8 7 6 5 4 3 2 1

This book is printed on acid-free paper.

All links and Web addresses were checked and verified to be correct at the time of publication. Because of the dynamic nature of the Web, some addresses and links may have changed since publication and may no longer be valid.

CONTENTS

The Tomb

The dawn of December 7, 1941, could not have been more peaceful. A soft breeze tugged gently at the palm trees while the placid blue water of the Pacific Ocean lapped at the beach. Oahu sat like a verdant gem in the brilliant necklace of the Hawaiian Islands. The entire place seemed to be at rest, yet nowhere was the Sunday-morning stillness so keenly felt as at Pearl Harbor. The home port of the United States Pacific Fleet was quiet and utterly unaware of what history had in store for it. Very soon, the peace of the day would be shattered and America would be at war.

Clouds hung over most of Oahu, breaking apart only here and there to reveal the azure sky. From the air, most of the island was hidden. Yet, strangely, the cloud cover disappeared directly above Pearl Harbor. The ships and aircraft at the naval base glittered in the bright sun. When they looked up, the sailors, soldiers, and airmen stationed at and around Pearl Harbor saw nothing but blue sky. This early—not even 8:00 a.m.—on a Sunday morning, however, not all of the base's servicemen were awake enough to notice nature's beauty. Some were asleep after a wild night on the town in Honolulu; others were drowsily pulling on their uniforms in preparation for an unwelcome shift of weekend duty. For others, church bells would soon call them to worship services.

Rumors about a possible war with Japan had been circulating. Everyone knew that the talks between the United States and its main rival in the Pacific had broken down over the issue of Japanese troops in China. Tensions were high, and it seemed likely that the diplomatic problems would be resolved through armed conflict. The officers and enlisted men at Pearl Harbor, however, like most Americans, imagined that war would come farther to the west, across the sea in the Philippines or the Dutch East Indies (today known as Indonesia). A young lieutenant stationed aboard the USS *Farragut* remembered how his ship "received several warnings from Washington" concerning a Japanese attack. He and his shipmates were well aware that the Japanese preferred to begin wars with surprise attacks on weekend mornings, but, as Lieutenant James Benham remembered, "At Pearl? Never! Too far away. The Philippines, Singapore, or even Indonesia. . . . But [none] of us expected a Japanese strike at Pearl."[1] Sitting nearly 3,000 miles from Japan, the men at the great naval base felt safe and secure.

No one sensed the danger that was growing around them. Even the warships at anchor in the harbor seemed at ease. Their slow swaying matched the relaxed, untroubled tempo of the sailors who began to move across their decks as the sun rose. Still, this was a military installation, and the dispute with Japan made security paramount. Fear of Japanese saboteurs and a keen desire to keep an eye on his ships led Admiral Husband E. Kimmel, the fleet commander, to arrange his vessels in neat rows so that they could be guarded more carefully. In case of a fight, Kimmel wanted his ships in one place and in one piece. The fleet was so well ordered and packed so closely together that, just the night before, Lieutenant General Walter Short, the Army commander in Hawaii, had marveled at the sight and remarked, "What a beautiful target that would make!"[2] Short had no idea that all too soon, the ships before him would become just that—a beautiful target.

The night of December 6 had passed uneventfully, and the next morning dawned quietly. Aboard the USS *Arizona*, nearly 1,000 officers and enlisted men went about their business. Suddenly, at 7:55 a.m., blaring Klaxons pierced the air, followed by a frantic alarm call—"General Quarters, this is no drill!"[3] Instantly, sailors tumbled out of their bunks, grabbed their combat gear, and raced to their battle stations. The sleepy *Arizona* sprang to life. Scurrying up from below decks, the men were greeted by a sight at once awesome and terrifying: The sky above them was filled with aircraft, all of them bearing the distinctive red-ball markings of the Imperial Japanese naval air forces.

More than 100 planes swirled in the air. Some dove, dropped their bombs, and then climbed, while their comrades who carried torpedoes swooped in low over the water, released their deadly cargo, and pulled up sharply. Higher up, nimble fighter planes turned in circles, providing protective cover for the dive bombers and torpedo planes, and periodically dropped down to strafe (fire machine guns on) the ships, buildings, and airfields of Pearl Harbor. Everywhere, explosives showered down on the Pacific fleet.

The well-trained Japanese pilots methodically sought out and attacked the American ships. Each of the pilots had been instructed on which warships to strike and how best to employ the weapons at his disposal. Bombs were dropped with pinpoint accuracy, punching holes in the decks of their targets. Torpedoes, specially designed for this mission to run shallow in the water, sliced into hulls before detonating. Massive

This is an undated aerial view of the USS *Arizona* battleship at sea in the Pacific with the crew on deck. The *Arizona*, one of the jewels in the U.S. Pacific Fleet moored at Pearl Harbor, was specifically targeted by Japanese pilots in the attack.

explosions wracked Pearl Harbor as one vessel after another burst into flame.

Soon, it was the *Arizona*'s turn. A Japanese pilot recognized the battleship, turned, and dove. Plummeting toward the *Arizona*, he released his bomb and pulled up into a steep climb. For a second, there was silence and then, as one of the *Arizona*'s men recalled, "a blinding flash. It was gigantic."[4] The lead Japanese pilot that morning recalled seeing a "hateful, mean-looking red flame" erupt skyward. He "knew at once that a big magazine had exploded."[5] An 800-kilogram (1,800-pound) bomb had penetrated the *Arizona*'s armored deck and struck its powder storage compartment, detonating tons of explosives. The ship's fuel tanks, adjacent to the magazine (the ammunition storeroom), ignited almost simultaneously. The huge vessel shuddered, lifted nearly 20 feet out of the water, and blew apart. One of the few survivors of the blast felt certain that, when "the *Arizona* exploded . . . they could have heard that noise back in California."[6] Sailors on surrounding ships were blown off the decks by the shock wave.

Built during World War I, the *Arizona* was perhaps the mightiest of the venerable "battlewagons," as sailors called them. At 608 feet long and 97 feet wide, the great ship weighed 31,400 tons. Its armor plating was 18 inches thick, and it mounted more than 40 guns of various types and calibers. The *Arizona* belonged to that class of warships that many people believed were virtually unsinkable. Now, in a moment, the ship had been transformed into a blazing tangle of twisted metal and dead bodies, a devastated hulk sinking slowly into the harbor.

As fires continued to burn on what was left of the *Arizona*, the water around it flared into a bright orange inferno. Burning oil spilled out of the doomed wreck, searing the desperate sailors who had jumped from its decks. Follow-up attacks by other Japanese planes touched off secondary explosions that tore at the *Arizona*. Bulkheads and supports collapsed. Topside superstructures literally fell into the gaping hole that had been opened by the initial blast. The two forward gun turrets tumbled more than 20 feet into the *Arizona*'s flaming interior.

All over Pearl Harbor, bombs fell from the sky and Japanese torpedoes streaked through the oily water. The sounds of war were deafening: The hellish roar of explosions blended with the growling of airplane engines and the harsh rattle of antiaircraft guns. Brave sailors from other ships attempted to rescue any survivors on board the doomed battleship, but it was no use. The captain and nearly his entire crew were already dead.

Smoke pours out of the battleship USS *Arizona* as it topples over into the sea during the attack on Pearl Harbor. The ship sank with more than 80 percent of its 1,500-man crew, including Rear Admiral Isaac C. Kidd. The attack broke the backbone of the U.S. Pacific Fleet and forced America out of a policy of isolationism.

Still the Japanese came. One torpedo, or perhaps two, slammed into what was now the wreckage of the *Arizona*. As many as eight more bombs fell on it. Throughout the attack on Pearl Harbor, the Japanese specifically targeted the *Arizona*. The end finally came at 10:32 a.m., when the planes turned away and sped northward to the carriers awaiting their return. The vessel was all but unrecognizable as it slipped below the water; what had been a proud battleship became a tomb for the estimated 960 men left aboard.

As the Americans at Pearl Harbor mourned, the Japanese pilots celebrated their success. Weary from battle, they congratulated themselves on having sunk or severely damaged 19 American warships, in addition to hundreds of U.S. aircraft that had been destroyed in simultaneous raids on Hawaiian airfields. None of the day's victories proved so satisfying to report as the obliteration of the *Arizona*, however: The after-action reports filed by the Japanese crews recounted the agonizing demise of the ship. One of the destroyer squadrons that accompanied the Japanese task force put the flyers' triumph in dry military language: ". . . Arizona broken out of her hull with torpedoes and bombs."[7]

Today, an elegant yet profoundly evocative memorial sits above the remnants of the shattered battleship. Stripped of its remaining masts, superstructure, and salvageable armaments, the *Arizona* rests on the floor of Pearl Harbor. Salvage efforts were considered in 1942, but the damage to the vessel was too extensive. Unlike most of the other ships sunk on December 7, the *Arizona* was beyond repair, and the decision was made to leave it where it lay. Over the years, attempts to retrieve the bodies of the men who died aboard the ship were similarly considered and abandoned. The Navy eventually declared the sailors inside to be officially buried at sea. Their tour of duty on the *Arizona* would last forever, as would the memory of that fateful day in 1941, the day that then-president Franklin Delano Roosevelt (FDR) promised would "live in infamy"[8]—the day that America went to war.

Pacific Empires

In the 1800s, both Japan and America were rapidly and delib-
erately orienting their economies and foreign policies toward
the vast expanses of the Pacific. Japan had traditionally viewed
itself as a great Asian power, albeit one that preferred a large
degree of isolation, whereas the United States had recently
dedicated itself to westward expansion. Both looked seaward
for trade and commerce. The 1847 acquisition of California,
with its priceless port of San Francisco, offered the United
States an opportunity for lucrative business ties to China.
Emerging in the mid-nineteenth century from a long history
of self-imposed seclusion, Japan likewise looked toward China
in the hopes of building a modern economy. Two young and
energetic nations thus looked out from their shores, pursuing
similar goals at precisely the same time. This coincidence of

history put Japan and the United States on track to become Pacific empires and mortal enemies.

Japanese society had been aggressive and highly militarized since the rise of the samurai in the late twelfth century. The Gempei Wars (1180–1185) between two of Japan's greatest samurai clans resulted in the establishment of what has been described as an "independent warrior government"[1] that transformed the four home islands of Honshu, Hokkaido, Kyushu, and Shokoku into a fortress controlled by military leaders known as shoguns. These men, determined to tolerate no challenge to their authority even from the emperor himself, closed off Japan to foreign influences in the hopes of sustaining a feudal order that supported samurai rule. During the following centuries, Japan withdrew from the modern world and shrouded itself in mystery.

The impenetrable wall built by the shoguns and the emperors they had manipulated collapsed in July 1853, when the Americans arrived. Eight months earlier, President Millard Fillmore had informed Congress that, acting as commander-in-chief, he had ordered "an appropriate naval force to Japan," in order to bring fundamental changes to "the inhospitable and anti-social system which it has pursued for about two centuries."[2] The American president hoped to pry open the tightly shut country and, in the process, open Asia to American culture, trade, and long-term resource exploitation. President Fillmore assigned this weighty task to Commodore Matthew Perry.

Perry and a small fleet appeared in Tokyo Bay in the summer of 1853. In an instant, Japan's history was irreversibly altered. The United States, quickly followed by Great Britain, forced trade concessions out of Japan almost immediately, backing up its demands with the threat of naval bombardment. This early use of naval power as a form of intimidation was not lost on the Japanese military elite as they stood by, helpless to

Above is a traditional Japanese illustration from the 1840s, of an event during the Gempei Wars in twelfth-century Japan. The print shows a warrior, wearing protective padded armor from which several arrows are protruding, prostrating himself onboard a ship. He is reporting to his emperor and others during the Battle of Dannoura.

respond. Within 15 years, with the support of the United States, the Meiji emperor had regained control of Japan and the office of shogun had been erased from the political structure. The old ways died hard, and many samurai refused to find a place in a modern Japan. Rebellion broke out, but such efforts to turn back the clock proved futile. The last embers of samurai resistance were extinguished in September 1877, with the failure of the Satsuma Rebellion.

Japan's imperial program of modernization and Westernization accelerated after the suppression of the samurai. The warrior ethos, the ancient Code of Bushido, however, found devotees among the officer class of Japan's new army and navy. These officers and the men they led stood in the vanguard of Japan's development between 1853 and 1890. During this period, Japan made a speedy transition from a closed feudal kingdom rooted in tradition to a modern state bent on regional expansion. Trade expanded rapidly in scope and scale. Imports and exports surged, as did rates of European investment. Japan's military establishment followed suit. The army and navy quickly gained lost ground, adopting European forms of organization, tactics, and weaponry in a race to become Asia's preeminent armed forces.

On every front, Japan advanced, but the speed of its transformation created a host of new problems. The population of the home islands grew, and cities became larger and denser. More people meant more mouths to feed and increasing pressure on a national food supply already inadequate for the demands placed on it. Industrialization only made matters worse. The factories required for modern production of building materials, machinery, consumer goods, and armaments for the army and navy absorbed vast quantities of raw materials, most of which were either scarce or altogether unavailable in Japan. Overall growth and the resulting demand for resources generated an expansionist impulse that led to militarism. The

This photograph of Commodore Matthew C. Perry was taken in the 1850s, around the time that Perry led the naval expedition to Japan (1852–1854) which compelled the nation to enter into diplomatic negotiations with the United States and to allow trading rights.

entire Pacific region thus became a stage on which Japan was destined to act in response to the challenges of modernity.

By 1890, Japan had very nearly completed its transition and stood ready to enter the imperial arena. Meanwhile, across the blue expanse of the Pacific Ocean, 6,000 miles away, another young imperial giant was stirring. The United States, long considered politically, socially, and culturally immature by European standards, had embarked on its own unique journey of transformation. For more than 200 years, America had been a frontier nation, characterized by farms, cattle, and Indian wars. By the last decade of the nineteenth century, however, the wild, youthful days of rapid continental expansion had ended. America was fast becoming a nation of cities and factories. By the end of the nineteenth century, the United States had come so far from its early roots that historian Frederick Jackson Turner felt compelled to declare that "the wilderness had been interpenetrated by lines of civilization growing ever more numerous."[3] In other words, the frontier had closed. America's traditional outlet for its expansionist urges no longer existed. The country's future lay abroad.

Much like Japan, the United States cast its glance toward the Pacific, where, since the first years of the republic, America had taken an interest in trade. The nation's first Asian expedition, in fact, took the form of a visit to China in 1784 by the aptly named ship *Empress of China*. The goal of the mission was to explore the economic potential of Eastern markets. Only after the bloody American Civil War, however, did the appropriate political and economic conditions for overseas development exist. The war accelerated demographic and industrial changes that had begun to reshape America as early as the 1820s and 1830s. Rising population rates, urbanization, and factory production were all accepted realities before the Civil War, but only after the peace in 1865 did the American landscape feel their full impact. Before the wounds of war had healed, telegraph lines and railroad tracks crisscrossed the nation. New and exciting technological advances seemed to be made almost every day. Electric lighting, telephones, and phonographs all led many people to agree with a contributor to *Scribner's* magazine in 1879 who asked, "If this can be done . . . what is there that cannot be?"[4]

Immigration swelled the urban Eastern states, prompting Americans to move westward in ever greater numbers. The subsequent exploitation of the West's grain, cattle, and mineral resources stimulated the national economy. As the economy soared, it also turned toward the Pacific. Famed for its role in channeling Sierra gold and silver into the vaults of New York banks, San Francisco established itself as the eastern terminus of a potential commercial line that would extend across the Pacific, a line punctuated by island stepping-stones such as Hawaii.

Lying almost equidistant between California and China, the Hawaiian Islands were recognized as crucial to America's transoceanic future as early as the 1870s. With the Philippines, Hawaii constituted a vital plank in the larger bridge to Asia. American whaling ships certainly appreciated Hawaii's value as a supply and repair depot. Such vessels depended on calls at Hawaii, the island of Oahu in particular, to refit and take on fresh food and water. In terms of global trade, however, Hawaii's real significance lay in its use as a coaling station for ships that were just beginning to make the switch from sails to coal-fired steam engines. Acting competitively, the United States negotiated a treaty with the islands' King Kalakaua in 1875 to deny the use of his finest port, Pearl Harbor, to the major European shipping powers. Twelve years later, a second treaty gave the United States exclusive rights to use Pearl Harbor as a port of call for American shipping.

As it inched its way toward China, the United States gradually came to see Japan as a serious competitor. The two nations' spheres of influence were fast approaching an intersection of sorts. Both viewed the exploitation of China as an economic and geopolitical necessity, and both knew that only vigorous moves to secure a hold on China's markets and resources would provide for future stability and prosperity. One such move, at least for the United States, had to be gaining not just access to but complete control over Hawaii. Consequently, the U.S. government supported an 1893 coup that seemed likely to lead to the direct annexation of the islands. Instead, an independent republic emerged in 1894, but it was administered by American businessmen who needed a mainland market for their sugar and pineapples. Through their domination, Hawaii became an American possession in all but name. At the same time, Japan defeated China after a brief war that allowed the Japanese to wring trade concessions from China. The Hawaiian takeover and the first Sino-Japanese War of 1894–1895 signalled the imperial intentions of the United States and Japan.

Japan had no time to rest after its victory over China before the United States made the next move in the imperial game. Hoping to secure additional links to China, the United States declared war on Spain in 1898. After a war that lasted only a few months, America seized Cuba, Guam, and the Philippines. Hawaii was openly annexed at the same time. The American success in taking possession of the most valuable part of Spain's decaying empire put the United States in a position to challenge the European states, many of which already had colonial enclaves in China. It also brought Japan and America into direct imperial contact for the first time. The word *enemy* was whispered with increasing frequency on both sides of the ocean. The stunning and wholly unexpected Japanese triumph in the Russo-Japanese War (1904–1905) increased the tension and suspicion even further. By launching an early morning surprise attack of torpedoes against the Russian fleet at anchor in Port Arthur in Manchuria, the Japanese navy destroyed Russian power in the Far East in a single stroke. Japanese forces also defeated a Russian task force sent to regain a lost outpost in the

Tsushima Strait, reinforcing the Russian humiliation and the Japanese victory.

The crushing blow against one of Europe's premier empires stunned the global military community and attested to the advanced state of Japanese military development. Certainly President Theodore Roosevelt felt new respect for Japan as he mediated the 1905 peace talks between the Asian nation and Russia held at Portsmouth, New Hampshire. Roosevelt called Japan's audacity "bully."[5] The president marveled at the way in which the Japanese navy caught the Russians napping at Port Arthur and smashed not only the fleet stationed there but also the relief force sent from Russia. He thus ensured that the peace treaty recognized Japan's mastery of the Korean peninsula and its special rights to trade in Manchuria, the primary objectives of the war with Russia. Although the Portsmouth treaty did not satisfy all of Japan's demands, especially the request for money from the Russians, it did explicitly acknowledge Japan's status as a regional power. The Japanese reciprocated later by accepting American control of the Philippines.

Not everyone shared Roosevelt's newfound admiration for the Japanese, however. Anti-Asian feelings were strong in the United States, particularly in the Western states. Throughout the nineteenth century, that hostility had been directed toward Chinese immigrants. The Japanese government felt no small amount of pride at the fact that Japanese immigrants in America experienced better treatment. Unlike the Chinese, who endured harsh discrimination and were subject to laws that were designed to keep them out, such as the Chinese Exclusion Act of 1882, Japanese enjoyed an elevated position among Asians in America. For this reason, the Japanese at home and in the United States were quite sensitive to anything that might seem insulting to their privilege.

The object lesson in Japanese sensibilities came in 1906, when the city of San Francisco moved to bring its Japanese residents down to what the city government considered to be

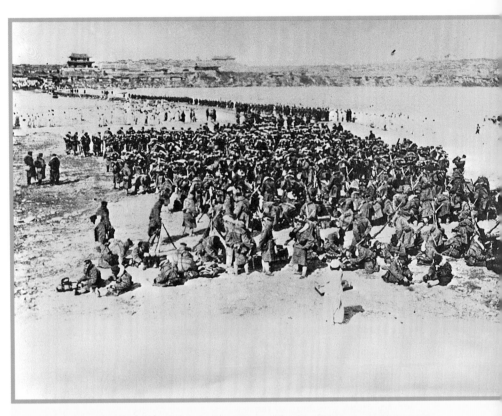

At the end of the nineteenth century and beginning of the twentieth, both the Russian and Japanese empires wanted to expand into Manchuria and Korea. Most observers expected the more powerful Russian army to rout the fledging Japanese military, but the smaller nation triumphed. Above, Japanese troops wait to cross the river at Ping Yang during the Russo-Japanese war of 1904, which was also the beginning of Japanese dominance in China.

their proper place. At precisely the same time that Congress was considering legislation to extend exclusion to Japanese immigrants, San Francisco ordered Japanese children to attend Chinese schools. Japanese boys and girls would no longer be allowed to attend schools that served white students.

The Japanese government reacted to the developments in Washington, D.C., and San Francisco with a fury that surprised everyone. The government in Tokyo demanded that President Roosevelt reject congressional calls for mandatory immigration restrictions and that he force San Francisco to rescind its school order. Rumors that Japan was considering war if the United States did not comply helped convince Roosevelt to do both. The president called the mayor of San Francisco and the entire city school board to Washington, D.C., where he personally ordered that Japanese students be allowed to attend white schools. He then silenced the voices in Congress that were calling for Japanese exclusion. In return, Japan accepted a

THEODORE ROOSEVELT
(1858–1919)

U.S. President, 1901–1909

With the exception of his distant relative Franklin Delano Roosevelt, no American president of the early twentieth century played a more active role in U.S.-Japanese relations than Theodore Roosevelt. Born in New York in 1858, "Teedie," as his family called him, possessed a burning curiosity about the world from his earliest days. Even as a young child, coping with asthma and a cool, distant father, Roosevelt was driven to explore the natural and human environments that surrounded him. As he grew into adulthood, Roosevelt developed a passion for science that was soon complemented by a strong inclination toward politics and history. Roosevelt graduated from Harvard University in 1880 and went on to a life that included travel abroad, two marriages, and a post as undersecretary of the Navy.

In 1898, Roosevelt experienced military service during the Spanish-American War as the commander of the famous Rough Riders cavalry unit. The war with Spain served as Roosevelt's introduction to American expansionism, a cause he embraced quickly "gentleman's agreement" by which they agreed to a voluntary policy "of discouraging immigration of its subjects . . . to the continental United States," and, in some cases, Hawaii.[6]

The international crisis of 1906–1907 passed, but the sour taste it left in the mouths of political leaders on both sides of the Pacific lingered. The possibility of war at some point in the future became obvious to the American military, so much so that it devised a special plan for dealing with a challenge from Japan—War Plan Orange. A comprehensive outline for operations in the Pacific, War Plan Orange presumed that hostilities

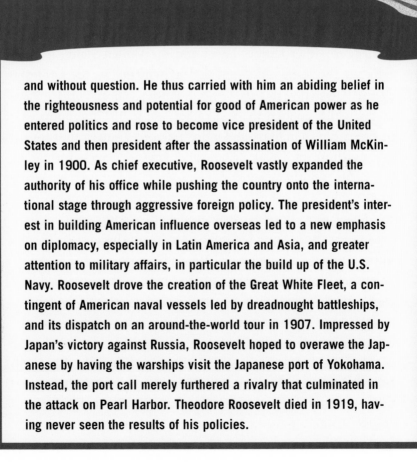

and without question. He thus carried with him an abiding belief in the righteousness and potential for good of American power as he entered politics and rose to become vice president of the United States and then president after the assassination of William McKinley in 1900. As chief executive, Roosevelt vastly expanded the authority of his office while pushing the country onto the international stage through aggressive foreign policy. The president's interest in building American influence overseas led to a new emphasis on diplomacy, especially in Latin America and Asia, and greater attention to military affairs, in particular the build up of the U.S. Navy. Roosevelt drove the creation of the Great White Fleet, a contingent of American naval vessels led by dreadnought battleships, and its dispatch on an around-the-world tour in 1907. Impressed by Japan's victory against Russia, Roosevelt hoped to overawe the Japanese by having the warships visit the Japanese port of Yokohama. Instead, the port call merely furthered a rivalry that culminated in the attack on Pearl Harbor. Theodore Roosevelt died in 1919, having never seen the results of his policies.

with Japan would necessarily include an attack on Pearl Harbor. The Port Arthur raid had been devastatingly successful, and American planners felt certain that the Japanese might someday try to repeat their success against the American installation in Hawaii. Japan took for granted that the United States was now more of an adversary than a mere competitor. Beginning in 1909, Japanese war planners focused on the U.S. naval base at Pearl Harbor, a port facility that would provide crucial support to any American fleet that sailed from California to Asian waters. Destroy Pearl Harbor and the United States would be evicted from the Pacific. By no later than 1910, therefore, both the United States and Japan were anticipating war with one another. The stage was being set for the events of December 7, 1941.

World War I (1914–1918) did nothing to alter military strategy in either nation. Japan and the United States, ironically on the same side, emerged as winners in the contest against Germany and its Central Powers allies. The United States, which entered the war rather late in 1917, announced its presence as a military and industrial force. American troops, joining those of Great Britain and France, helped turn the tide of the fighting against the Germans on Europe's western front, while American factories provided crucial supplies for the Allied war effort. Japan gained both territory and influence in East Asia. Long before the Americans became involved in the conflict, in September 1914, the Japanese seized China's Shantung Peninsula, a parcel of land previously controlled by Germany. Four months later, they issued a series of demands to the Chinese government that effectively gave Japan special economic privileges in China and the right to defend those privileges with Japanese troops if need be. When the Chinese balked at what are known as the Twenty-one Demands, Japan threatened military action. China eventually relented and, over American objections, in May 1915, gave Japan the economic and military concessions it had requested.

The Twenty-one Demands sent a signal to the United States that Japan considered itself the rightful dominant power in Asia. The American military contribution to the Allied cause convinced the Japanese that the United States had the strength to assert its will when it chose to do so. Moreover, the German surrender in 1918 and the subsequent peace treaty that stripped Germany of its overseas possessions removed that country from the power equation in the Pacific region. Similarly, the exhaustion of Britain and France, after four long years of bitter fighting, reduced their ability to shape developments in the Far East, and internal revolution in Russia meant that it could no longer influence events in Asia as it had earlier in the century. In all, the end of World War I saw the United States and Japan as the only legitimate contestants for dominance in the Pacific and China. The course toward a possible war was set, but not irreversibly. The likelihood of some kind of accommodation still existed, at least in the years immediately after World War I. All of that would change during the 1920s and 1930s, as the United States and Japan grew stronger and new wars erupted in Asia and Europe.

War Clouds
Gather

Friction between Japan and the United States increased during the 1920s. Each nation sought accommodation from the other and hoped that future conflict could be avoided, but the borders of their expanding spheres of influence in the Pacific were nearing a collision point at which only war could settle matters once and for all. From November 1921 to February 1922, the United States hosted delegates from nine countries in a conference to work toward naval disarmament, specifically to establish firm limits on the size of the navies that could be put on the high seas during peacetime. The hope at the conclusion of the meeting was for balance, stability, and future peace. The agreement reached by the delegates, however, had just the opposite effect. The limitations they determined put Japan at a distinct disadvantage relative to the United States and Great Britain.

The Japanese had nursed a sense of wounded national pride since the Paris Peace Conference of 1919, at which, they felt, they had been cheated out of the full value of their role in helping to defeat Germany. They chalked this up to racism and the West's desire to keep Japan from realizing its political and military potential in Asia. That suspicion was confirmed in Japanese eyes when the Washington conferees settled on a sliding scale of limitations that gave different nations different caps on the numbers of warships that could be built. According to that scale, Japan could possess more ships, measured in tons, than either Italy or France but far fewer than Great Britain and the United States.

The so-called 5:5:3 ratio (500,000 tons each for the United States and Britain and 300,000 tons for Japan) insulted Japanese honor and belittled the empire in the eyes of the global military community by seeming to lump it with the least of the major powers in Europe. The Japanese craved the sort of recognition that equality with Britain and the United States would have given them. Japanese leaders, especially in the military, were convinced that the discriminatory naval arrangements devised in Washington, D.C., were an attempt to bully Japan off the seas and cripple its ability to expand in Asia. So sure were the Japanese of latent American hostility that the instructors at the Eta Jima naval academy began to teach their students that the United States would very soon become the enemy of Japan.

Even ordinary sailors and soldiers began to take eventual war with America to be a given fact. When a group of Japanese midshipmen sailed into San Francisco Bay in 1924 on a training cruise, one of the first things they did was to inspect the American vessels at anchor there. One of them, a future pilot, paid close attention to the deck and hull armor of the battleship USS *Maryland*. Scrutinizing the *Maryland*, the young sailor wondered "when he might be called upon to bomb or torpedo that ship."[1] His name was Mitsuo Fuchida; 17 years later, he would be at the controls of the lead plane in the attack on Pearl Harbor.

American military planners understood, no less than their Japanese counterparts, the need to prepare for a possible war in the Pacific. It seemed logical to presume that Pearl Harbor would be one of Japan's first targets should such a war break out. Indeed, Brigadier General Billy Mitchell, a pioneer in military aviation, made a startling prediction only two years after the Washington Naval Disarmament Conference. After returning from a tour of Asia in 1924, Mitchell wrote a report for the War Department that stressed that a war with Japan would almost certainly begin with a surprise attack on Pearl Harbor. The general surmised that the destruction of Pearl Harbor would prevent American ships from reaching East Asian waters to challenge the Japanese there. This, in turn, would give the Japanese navy a free hand for many months while Pearl Harbor was being repaired. By the time an American fleet could sail into the western Pacific, the Japanese would be waiting for them, ready to fight what the Japanese called the "Great All-Out Battle," a winner-take-all contest between the Japanese and American main forces.

The U.S. Navy took the findings of Mitchell's report seriously enough to test it out in sea exercises. In 1928, aircraft flying from the deck of the aircraft carrier USS *Langley* launched a mock air raid against Pearl Harbor with the express purpose of determining whether such an attack was possible. It was. That same year, a Japanese naval officer named Isoroku Yamamoto gave a lecture at the Japanese naval academy in which he argued that it was possible to use torpedoes, dropped from airplanes, to attack warships at anchor in a military port. It would be difficult, he noted, and the element of surprise was crucial. Drawing partly on the example of the successful raid on Port Arthur in 1904, Yamamoto claimed that such an attack could

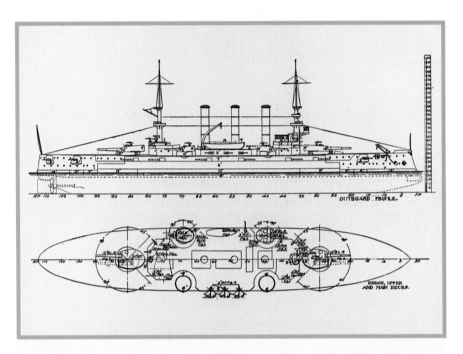

The plans above show the ship USS *Connecticut*, the leading ship in its class at the time, in profile and from a birds-eye view. When a group of Japanese midshipmen sailed into San Francisco Bay in 1924 on a training cruise, they inspected the American vessels at anchor there, paying close attention to the decks and hull armor of the battleships.

be carried out. Soon to become commander-in-chief of the Combined Fleet, Yamamoto would later put his theory to the test at Pearl Harbor.

Japan and the United States monitored each other very closely throughout the 1920s. This included the first American efforts (beginning in 1924) to break Japan's complex diplomatic and military codes. At the same time, Japan actively began to gather intelligence in the United States. The two sides also started reconsidering their objectives in the Pacific. For Japan, this meant thinking ahead toward a future in which it would be the region's sole power. The difficulty for Japan, one not shared by the United States, was the matter of securing the raw resources necessary for modern life. This made China the centerpiece of Japanese foreign policy in the late 1920s.

China possessed many of the material resources that Japan desperately needed, not only to achieve a modern standard of living but also to expand beyond its borders. Indeed, the Japanese economy could not support the existing imperial program of expansion, let alone push it further along. The global depression that began in the United States in 1929 did not help. Struggling in many economic sectors as it was, Japan was hit hard by the worldwide slowdown. More than ever, the country needed ready access to stocks of food and strategic materials such as iron ore, aluminum, rubber, and oil. Lacking these resources at home, Japan turned to China. It had hoped that the Twenty-one Demands would provide for at least some long-term economic stability, but China persisted in exercising what little sovereignty it had left after World War I. If Japan wanted what China had, in other words, the empire would have to take it, by force if need be.

The first step in this direction was taken in 1931. Claiming that their railroad line near Mukden, acquired as part of the Twenty-one Demands, had been attacked by Chinese troops, the Japanese moved to occupy Manchuria and take control of its harbors, railroads, soybean fields, and coal and iron mines. Attempting to camouflage this blatant aggression as a campaign of "liberation," the Japanese set up a puppet government in March 1932 and announced the establishment of the Republic of Manchukuo. Sunk in the depths of the Great Depression, the United States did nothing to stop them. In fact, when the Chinese sought American support in ousting the Japanese, Secretary of State Henry Stimson declined, saying that he wanted to make it clear that the government of President Herbert Hoover was "playing no favorites."[2]

Still, troubled by this occupation, Hoover and his secretary of state hoped that words would be enough to check Japan's expansion in China. Such a policy seemed to have worked in the past. Only two years earlier in fact, in 1930, a moderate government in Tokyo had accepted a continuation of the limits imposed by the Naval Disarmament Conference, and the Japanese assured the United States that they had no militaristic intentions beyond safeguarding their society and economy. The United States therefore felt confident that the Japanese would be satisfied with what they had gained in Manchuria and would take no further actions on the mainland. It was taken for granted that the Japanese would never be so bold as to move southward into China proper.

The Japanese military, the Imperial Army in particular, however, had been increasingly vocal and influential since the late 1920s. By 1936, some officers had become so certain of their ability to guide Japan to greatness that they planned and launched a coup against the nation's civilian government. The attempt failed miserably, but it allowed mainstream officers in the army and navy to claim that a state of emergency existed and to demand the inclusion of military men in the imperial cabinet. The military wanted a general to fill the post of war minister, and an admiral to serve in the office of navy minister, requests that were quickly granted. Using its newfound authority, the military began to lobby unceasingly for invasion of China. The conquest of the rest of China, the military argued, would secure vast amounts of material resources and a huge pool of labor for the empire.

America's reaction was the wild card. The Japanese government worried about the reaction of the Roosevelt administration to an invasion of China. As if to assure the civilian leadership of the military's foresight, the 1936 imperial war games included a simulated attack on Pearl Harbor. The cabinet and the emperor were assured that, if the Americans tried to intervene to stop a Chinese campaign, they would be defeated. The matter of an attack on Pearl Harbor deeply interested one of the navy attendees at the games. This young officer was Minoru Genda, a brilliant tactician who would later apply what he learned in theory to the very real plan for an attack on Hawaii, a plan he created.

The Japanese generals eventually won the day. In 1937, Japan invaded China, once again claiming that an attack had been made on its forces, this time at Marco Polo Bridge in Beijing. The American response now was anything but conciliatory. Although not seeking a confrontation outright, President Franklin Roosevelt made it clear that American patience with Japanese expansionism had it limits. In October 1937, the president told an audience in Chicago that international aggression was like a disease, and when "an epidemic of physical disease

FRANKLIN DELANO ROOSEVELT'S QUARANTINE SPEECH

By 1937, war was spreading in Europe and Asia. Hitler's Germany and Mussolini's Italy were actively supporting the Fascist rebellion in Spain with men and supplies while preparing for their own wars of aggression in the very near future. Meanwhile, Japanese troops had invaded China and were marching southward. At the same time, Japanese bombers were systematically laying waste to China's cities. Against this backdrop, President Franklin Roosevelt appealed to the "peace-loving nations" of the world to join together in opposition to expansionism. Careful to avoid directly naming Germany, Italy, and Japan for fear of increasing global tensions, Roosevelt stated openly in his 1937 Quarantine Speech that international security and stability could not be ensured until the contagion of war could be contained. Excerpts from the speech appear below.

. . . Without a declaration of war and without warning or justification of any kind, civilians, including vast numbers of women and starts to spread . . . [there must be] a quarantine of the patients in order to protect the health of the community. . . ."[3] Roosevelt put Japan on notice. Its growth would be contained, and the United States would do whatever it took to keep Japan from "plunging the whole world into war."[4]

Roosevelt's warnings fell on deaf ears. Notwithstanding American protests, the Japanese pressed their campaign in China and went so far as to attack and sink an American vessel, the USS *Panay*, in the Yangtze River. One of the pilots who led the attack was Lieutenant Shigeharu Murata; four years later, his 1st Torpedo Attack Unit would swoop down on Pearl Harbor and devastate the battleships gathered there. Murata was

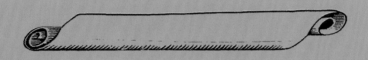

children, are being ruthlessly murdered with bombs from the air. In times of so-called peace, ships are being attacked and sunk by submarines without cause or notice. Nations are fomenting and taking sides in civil warfare in nations that have never done them any harm. Nations claiming freedom for themselves deny it to others. Innocent peoples, innocent nations, are being cruelly sacrificed to a greed for power and supremacy which is devoid of all sense of justice and humane considerations. The peace-loving nations must make a concerted effort in opposition to those violations of treaties and those ignorings [sic] of human instincts. . . . It seems to be unfortunately true that the epidemic of lawlessness is spreading . . . the peace of the world and the welfare and security of every nation, including our own, is today being threatened by that very thing.

*Paterson, *Major Problems,* pp. 173–175.

not a man to make errors in identification of military targets; still, the Japanese said that the *Panay* had been mistaken for a Chinese ship. This weak excuse did not convince many in Washington, D.C.: An apology and assurances against future "mistakes" were demanded and given.

The world was indeed fast becoming a dangerous place by the late 1930s. Japan's war in China was only one source of concern. In Europe, civil war raged in Spain. Nazi Germany had annexed Austria and absorbed the Sudetenland region of Czechoslovakia. By 1938, Adolf Hitler's armies were poised to take the rest of Czechoslovakia, and war with Poland seemed likely. Led by Benito Mussolini and his Fascists, Italy had invaded and conquered Ethiopia and announced its intention to resurrect the Roman Empire, at least in Africa and the Mediterranean area. The Soviet Union, meanwhile, had consolidated its power in Eurasia and declared the spread of communism to be its global mission. With millions of men in their armies, the Soviets had the manpower to back up their pronouncements with action. Japan was well aware of the threat posed by hundreds of Russian divisions stationed in Soviet Asia just north of China and thus moved to ally itself with Germany and Italy in an anti-Communist coalition.

Japan left no doubt in anyone's mind that it intended to protect itself and its interests. When war broke out in Europe in 1939 with Germany and Italy on one side and Great Britain and France on the other, Japan stepped up its military preparations for a conflict in the Pacific. This compelled the United States military to revise and refine its plans to counter Japan. The significance of Pearl Harbor within this context grew daily. Its port facilities would be vital in any attempt to take the Pacific Fleet from its base in California to a point in Asia where it could defend the Philippines and to bring the Japanese navy into battle. Pearl Harbor's strengths and weaknesses had to be reassessed in light of its strategic value. Toward that end, the U.S. Navy conducted sea exercises in which aircraft were launched against

This is an aerial photograph of Pearl Harbor on the island of Oahu before it was attacked. Oahu was considered a strategic base for the U.S. Navy, as it solidified the American presence in the Pacific Ocean.

Hawaii from the carrier USS *Saratoga*. The exercises proved that such an attack could devastate Pearl Harbor and jeopardize American control of the islands if the air raid were followed by the landing of Japanese troops. In May 1940, knowing that Japan posed a threat to Hawaii and perhaps even to California, President Roosevelt ordered the Pacific Fleet to move its home base permanently to Pearl Harbor. The fleet commander, Admiral James O. Richardson, objected strongly to the reassignment of his ships. He contended that Pearl Harbor lacked credible air defenses and was open to low-level torpedo attacks. He was promptly overruled, and his were concerns dismissed.

President Roosevelt's reasoning on the Pearl Harbor move was simple: If war came, he wanted his warships close enough to the Philippines to deter a Japanese invasion of the archipelago and to keep the Japanese from being tempted to move against either the Aleutian Islands in Alaska or the West Coast. Through all of this, however, Roosevelt continued to insist that diplomacy be considered the first line of defense in America's arsenal. He believed that a peaceful resolution of the growing tensions with Japan was possible. The president's hopes dimmed markedly, though, in the summer of 1940. German troops entered Paris that June, defeating France and giving Japan an opportunity to occupy Indochina, the premier French colony in Asia. Japan could use the bounty of Indochina's rice and rubber plantations and bolster the war effort in China by cutting the supply lines through the colony to the Chinese nationalist forces that were holding out in the south of the country.

The Imperial Army pounced quickly on the tender morsel left behind by the French. In July 1940, Japanese soldiers marched into and occupied northern French Indochina. Increasingly frustrated by Japanese ambitions, Roosevelt's government took action with speed and determination. The United States could not physically stop Japan from taking Indochina, but it certainly did not have to make the job any easier. Employing the only weapon it could at the time, the U.S. Congress imposed an embargo on exports of high-grade scrap metal and high-octane fuel to Japan. The Japanese war machine thus would neither run on American gasoline nor be built with recycled American metal. True, Japanese airplanes and vehicles could use the lower-octane fuel not included in the embargo and Japan had a reserve of factory-quality metal on hand, but the American message was read clearly in Tokyo. Two months after the occupation of Indochina, in September 1940, Japan signed a defense pact with Germany and Italy; it now officially belonged to a Berlin-Rome-Tokyo Axis that pledged each nation to come to the aid of any other that was attacked by a power *not* already fighting in Europe. This meant the United States.

At almost the same moment that the Japanese joined the Axis, American cryptologists successfully cracked the Japanese diplomatic cipher known as PURPLE using a top-secret technique that the Americans called "MAGIC." From then on, the United States had the ability to read every message sent from Tokyo to its embassy in Washington, D.C. From the MAGIC decryptions, the United States first learned of the Japanese navy's intense interest in the British attack on the Italian fleet at its anchorage at the port of Taranto. On November 11, 1940, 24 British torpedo planes took off from the carrier HMS *Illustrious.* By the time they returned, the Italian Mediterranean Fleet was either sinking or severely damaged. For the Japanese navy, which had long theorized that torpedoes could be air-dropped against warships at anchor, Taranto was an object lesson in the offensive power of naval aviation.

Japan quickly sent a team of naval analysts from its embassy in Rome to survey and report on the damage done by the British. Assigned at the time to the post of naval attaché in London, Lieutenant Commander Minoru Genda, the same Genda who had heard Yamamoto's torpedo lectures, listened to the news of Taranto with great interest. Genda had always believed in the marriage of the airplane and the torpedo; now, he was convinced that a war with the United States would have to involve both. Already, an idea was developing in Genda's mind. Like his friend Mitsuo Fuchida and Admiral Yamamoto, Genda began to picture a lightning strike against the American Pacific Fleet, using torpedo planes reinforced with dive bombers and level bombers, at its home port of Pearl Harbor. Destroy the fleet at Pearl Harbor at the very outset of hostilities, Genda thought, and Japan might just be able to win the war that many in Japan and the United States could sense approaching. The American secretary of the Navy, Frank Knox, would have agreed. Commenting on the significance of Taranto, Knox urged that "precautionary measures be taken immediately to protect Pearl Harbor against such a surprise attack in the event of war between the United States and Japan."[5]

With the U.S. Pacific Fleet out of action, perhaps all of East Asia could be brought under Japanese control within what the Japanese referred to as the Greater East Asia Co-Prosperity Sphere—in essence an expanded and virtually invincible empire that stretched from Manchuria to Indonesia. By December 1940, the stakes were growing in the dangerous game being played by the United States and Japan. Publicly, the United States continued to flex its rhetorical muscles. President Roosevelt told Americans that "three powerful nations, two in Europe and one in Asia" had joined together "in a program aimed at world control."[6] Although the United States was not at war yet, Roosevelt pledged that America would "be the great arsenal of democracy,"[7] giving the British all the material support it could. Germany, Italy, and Japan were warned—the United States stood against them in peace and, if necessary, in war. Privately, Roosevelt admitted that he did not "want to be drawn into a war with Japan."[8] German submarines were running wild in the Atlantic, sinking British merchant ships at will, and the president had to concentrate his available naval forces there. Despite Japanese actions in China and Indochina and despite the government's embargoes and his personal revulsion at Japanese aggression, Roosevelt could not afford to fight; he had to maintain the peace. Events, however, were conspiring to deny him that luxury.

Enter Yamamoto

By January 1941, relations between Japan and the United States were deteriorating rapidly. Japanese troops had taken up station in Indochina, and their government flatly refused to withdraw them. In retaliation, the United States extended the fuel and metal embargoes of July 1940 to include iron ore, copper, nickel, uranium, and oil drilling and refining equipment. Although President Roosevelt and many moderate politicians in Japan hoped for peace, some sort of military confrontation between the Pacific empires appeared more likely with each passing day. The only questions were where and when.

Along with many other political figures, the U.S. ambassador to Japan, Joseph Grew, worried intensely about the prospect of war. Like all diplomats, Grew preferred dialogue over force when it came to settling international disputes. Grew sensed that talking might not be enough this time, however. His fears were heightened in late January 1941, when he was told by a Peruvian diplomat that "a surprise attack on Pearl Harbor was planned by the Japanese military forces, in case of 'trouble' between Japan and the United States."[1] Of course, talk of a raid on Pearl Harbor was nothing new within military circles. Throughout the 1930s, according to Major General Sherman Miles, the operations officer for the Army's Hawaiian Department, the military expected "a surprise attack by the Japanese on Hawaii, made with little or no warning . . ." at the outset of any war in the Pacific.[2] The warning conveyed to Ambassador Grew, however, was much more precise and came at a much more dangerous moment in time.

Grew dutifully wired the State Department to pass along the Peruvian information, but his superiors felt that the source was too unreliable. The warning was dismissed. In Japan, however, plans for just such a strike were maturing quickly. Commander-in-Chief of the Combined Fleet Admiral Yamamoto, in fact, had already decided that the "most important thing we have to do first in a war with the U.S. . . . is to fiercely attack the U.S. main fleet" at Pearl Harbor.[3] Yamamoto had long supported the combination of aircraft and torpedoes for use in the type of surprise attack he had witnessed against Port Arthur during the Russo-Japanese War. Pearl Harbor, he felt, would be the place where Japan just might be able to achieve a second stunning naval victory and win another war against a Western power.

As Yamamoto's thinking became ever more tightly focused on Pearl Harbor, the American base changed commands. In February 1941, Admiral Richardson, never content with the move from California, was replaced by Admiral Husband Kimmel. Kimmel understood Pearl Harbor's vulnerabilities, but he was confident that he could defend the port and the ships stationed there. His optimism was shared by Lieutenant General Walter Short, the Army's new commander in Hawaii.

Short assured Kimmel that the fighter aircraft under his control were more than capable of securing Hawaii's skies and that his troops could repel any attempted invasion. The general was so sure of himself that, on his way to Hawaii to assume his command, Short read a novel instead of briefing papers on the situation in the Pacific with special regard to Japan. Both Kimmel and Short felt that Hawaii was safe.

Yamamoto hoped to make it much less so. The admiral imagined Hawaii to be "a dagger aimed at the throat of Japan,"[4] a dagger he was determined to blunt at the very beginning of a war with the United States. "In the event of war with the United States," Yamamoto wrote to Rear Admiral Takijiro Onishi, chief of staff of the 11th Air Fleet, in February 1941, "we [must] deal a crushing blow to the main force of the American fleet in Hawaiian waters. . . ."[5] Thus, he ordered Onishi to study the feasibility of an attack on Pearl Harbor. Onishi, in turn, assigned the task to Commander Minoru Genda.

Genda had learned a great deal from his study of naval aviation and the British attack on Taranto. He believed strongly that the type of operation envisioned by Yamamoto could be carried out only by a massive aircraft carrier task force that sailed secretly from Japanese home waters and struck on a day and at a time when the Americans least expected it. Intrigued by the challenge of putting together the plans for such a mission, Genda accepted the assignment and went to work.

The commander finished his job in record time. By the end of February, Genda had devised a daring plan for a surprise attack on the U.S. Pacific Fleet. He proposed that a task force consisting of three carrier divisions, six aircraft carriers in all, sail quietly along a northern approach route toward Hawaii. When it reached its destination, the task force would launch two strike waves that totaled 300 planes against Pearl Harbor. Using a combination of torpedoes, dive bombs, level bombs, and machine guns, the aircraft would target, in order of priority, the American aircraft carriers, battleships, land-based

Admiral Isoroku Yamamoto, commander of Japan's Combined Fleet, is shown in Japan on December 12, 1941. In a lecture at the Japanese naval academy, Yamamoto argued that it was possible to use torpedoes, dropped from airplanes, to attack warships at anchor in a military port. He later orchestrated the attack on Pearl Harbor.

fighter and scout planes, and auxiliary ships. Genda emphasized the need for complete secrecy. The task force would have to arrive in Hawaiian waters undetected, and he agreed with Yamamoto that the damage to Pearl Harbor had to guarantee its uselessness to the U.S. Navy for at least six months. This would give the Japanese army enough time to follow up with the operations it was planning in the southwestern Pacific, campaigns designed to secure reliable sources of raw materials for Japan.

As Genda presented his blueprint to Rear Admiral Onishi, he stressed two things above all else. First, he insisted on the absolute need for the task force to hunt down the three American carriers that were assigned to the Pacific. Genda argued that these ships posed the gravest threat to ongoing Japanese offensive operations. Second, he reiterated the fact that the Japanese carriers had to follow a northerly route in order to avoid detection by "American reconnaissance planes from Hawaii [which] were thick in the southern area."[6] Onishi asked Genda whether a total victory would result from an attack on Pearl Harbor. Genda replied that the Americans had the ability to raise and repair ships sunk there, because the water was so shallow. "For this reason," Genda replied, "we could not expect a great success in this attack." Would the operation work, Onishi demanded, pushing Genda to take a firm position. Genda explained in summation that an attack on Pearl Harbor and the elimination of the American fleet for at least six months "while extremely difficult, is not impossible."[7] With that, Operation Hawaii, as the Japanese called it, was given the go-ahead.

Back in Hawaii, the new American commanders were settling in and commissioning reports. Both Kimmel and Short began to assess the threats that they faced. One of these reports, authored jointly by Major General Frederick Martin and Rear Admiral Patrick Bellinger, warned that, if relations between Japan and the United States deteriorated sufficiently, the Japanese would most likely launch a surprise dawn attack against Pearl Harbor. The officers further predicted that the carriers from which the strike would be dispatched would put Japanese planes in the air from a position 300 miles out to sea.

This report received added credibility from Admiral Harold Stark, the chief of naval operations. Stark had sent a message to Kimmel on April 1, 1941, just days before Martin and

Bellinger offered their study for consideration. "Personnel of your naval intelligence service," Stark wrote, "should be advised that because of the fact that past experience shows the [Japanese] often begin activities in a particular field on Saturdays and Sundays [Pearl Harbor should] take steps on such days to see that proper watches and precautions are in effect."[8]

Taken together, everything pointed to a carrier-borne surprise attack on Pearl Harbor launched on a weekend after a collapse of diplomatic relations and at the very beginning of a war. Kimmel and Short had been advised to prepare for exactly the type of assault that Yamamoto, Genda, and the Combined Fleet were planning. Neither man, however, took the warning signs to heart or fully appreciated their implications. Part of the explanation for this lay in the popular military wisdom of the day, which held that Pearl Harbor was too far away from Japan to be in immediate danger, even from carrier-borne attacks. Kimmel's and Short's failure also could be attributed to the general lack of respect for Japanese military prowess that was common among American officers in 1941. Although they anticipated future hostile action by Japan, many American military planners shared the sentiments of war analyst Fletcher Pratt, who claimed in 1939 that the Japanese "can neither make good planes nor fly them well."[9] The Japanese, Pratt concluded, were simply "poor aviators."[10] Similarly, the assistant U.S. naval attaché in Tokyo boasted, "We can lick the Japs in twenty-four hours."[11] In March 1941, a reporter perhaps summed up the informal military attitude best when he noted that "naval people hold the Japanese to be very inferior . . . [they] feel we should have knocked off the little brown brother years ago. . . ."[12]

While the Americans were busying themselves first recognizing and then discounting the Japanese threat, the emperor's army was bogged down in China and the home islands were feeling the full effects of the 1940 embargoes. China had technically fallen to the Japanese, but Chinese forces remained in the

Admiral Husband E. Kimmel (above) became the commander in chief of the U.S. Pacific Fleet in February 1941. On November 27, 1941, Kimmel fortunately dispatched carrier task forces from Pearl Harbor to deliver marine aircraft to bases on Wake and Midway islands. Consequently, the Japanese attack deprived the Pacific Fleet only of its battleships. Still the attack stunned the United States and its navy, and the Roosevelt administration made Kimmel a scapegoat.

field. The Nationalist armies, led by General Chiang Kai-shek, held most of the southern areas; Chinese Communists, under the command of Mao Tse-Tung, harassed Japanese occupation troops in central China. Only in Manchuria and the cities was the Japanese hold secure. The war that began in 1937 and should have ended rather quickly continued to rage in 1941. The Imperial Army therefore stepped up its demands for war supplies. The problem was the U.S. embargoes. The army needed metal and fuel above all else, and the United States was no longer providing these. Japan would have to look elsewhere and, according to an April 1941 army report, the only place where supplies existed in sufficient amounts was the southwestern Pacific, specifically in the colonies then administered by Great Britain and the Netherlands.

In this vast stretch of territory that reached from Japanese-occupied Indochina across British Malaya to the Dutch East Indies (Indonesia) lay everything Japan needed—rice, metals, rubber, and, most important, oil. Control of this area, under the guise of building the Co-Prosperity Sphere, would guarantee Japan the self-sufficiency it needed to win the war in China and pursue its policy of creating an enduring Japanese empire throughout East Asia. To achieve these ends, the British, the Dutch, and the Americans would have to be fought.

Although supportive of the goal of expansion and, ultimately, war with the United States and Great Britain, the Japanese navy generally found itself at odds with the army as to the timing of future operations. Many fleet officers, however prepared to fight, worried that the moment for a major conflict with the United States had not yet arrived. They particularly doubted the wisdom of an attack on Pearl Harbor such as the one that Yamamoto and Genda were devising. Yamamoto understood their uneasiness, but he disagreed about the issue of timing. The American fleet posed an unparalleled danger to Japan and its long-term economic and political goals, the admiral argued. Pearl Harbor had to be neutralized, and the sooner the better. Yamamoto reminded his more reluctant staff officers that the U.S. Navy was currently spread very thin, having to assign ships to support the British in the Atlantic as the latter battled the German U-boats. America could not fully commit all of its naval assets to a war with Japan, which gave Japan the advantage, though only momentarily. Yamamoto's assessment was quite accurate. President Roosevelt himself had admitted privately in June 1941 that he did not "have enough Navy to go around—and every little episode in the Pacific

A Japanese infantry unit gets ready to battle against the Chinese Communist Armed Forces in China during the Second Sino-Japanese War in August 1937. At the time, Japan was striving to create an empire that would control much of East Asia.

means fewer ships in the Atlantic."[13] There would never be a better opportunity for Japan to strike, if it indeed had to.

Roosevelt needed peace in the Pacific even more than Yamamoto suspected. The president dreaded any more "episodes" that might distract the United States from concentrating on giving assistance to the British. In July 1941, President Roosevelt got exactly what he did not want. The Japanese army moved to occupy southern Indochina, and America had to respond. Roosevelt's government did so by effectively embargoing crude oil shipments to Japan and freezing all Japanese assets in American banks. Until that point, Japan had imported 88 percent of its crude oil, nearly every drop of it from the United States. Without access to money deposited in the United States, furthermore, Japan could not purchase any number of vital goods on the open market. Combined with the earlier embargoes on metal and refined fuel, the restrictions imposed by the Roosevelt administration confronted Japan with the very real prospect of having its economy ruined and its military machine stopped. Unless its diplomats in Washington could broker a deal to have the embargoes lifted, Japan would be left with only one alternative: war.

The Imperial Army seized on the embargoes as a pretext for the southern campaign it had lobbied for since early 1940. The Japanese government, however, led by Prime Minister Fumimaro Konoye, counseled patience. Konoye instructed the

ISOROKU YAMAMOTO
(1884–1943)

Architect of the Attack

Admiral Isoroku Yamamoto, the man who developed and oversaw the implementation of the plan to attack Pearl Harbor, was born on April 4, 1884. The son of a former samurai, Yamamoto gave himself over to a career at sea as a young man, when he entered the Japanese Naval Academy. Yamamoto graduated in 1904, served during the Russo-Japanese War, and fought bravely at the battle of Tsushima Strait. After recovering from wounds suffered in that engagement (he lost two fingers on his left hand), he went to the United States to study at Harvard University. There, Yamamoto learned to respect American courage and tenacity. He also came to the conclusion that the United States was Japan's most likely adversary in the decades to come.

During the 1920s, Yamamoto became a tireless advocate of naval air power, arguing for a rapid buildup of the Japanese aircraft carrier fleet. He was especially keen on the idea of combining the emerging torpedo technology with the type of surprise attack the Japanese had famously carried out against the Russians at Port

Japanese ambassador to the United States, the former admiral Kichisaburo Nomura, to open talks with his American counterpart, Secretary of State Cordell Hull. Splitting the difference between the army and the government, Yamamoto supported negotiations but nonetheless stood ready to go forward with Operation Hawaii. If negotiations with the Americans failed, Genda's outline for an attack on the Pacific fleet would be revised into a working battle plan.

The Japanese army and navy were ready to move. Despite their differences, both services were confident that they could

Arthur in 1904. This was the genesis of Operation Hawaii. After serving as Japan's naval attaché in Washington (1926–1928) and deputy navy minister (1936), Yamamoto was promoted to the rank of admiral and became the commander in chief of the Combined Fleet in 1940. The next year, Pearl Harbor made Yamamoto a hero in Japan, but the admiral still thought of himself as simply an officer doing his duty. The failed attack on the Midway Islands in June 1942 did nothing to dull the luster of his fame.

Neither did his habitual gambling nor his love affair with a geisha girl named Chiyoko, to whom he wrote many warm and revealing letters during the war. It was to Chiyoko that one of Admiral Yamamoto's officers went on May 20, 1943, to say, "I am very sorry to tell you the sad and unexpected news. . . ."* The architect of Japan's triumph at Pearl Harbor had fallen in battle. While on an inspection tour of Japanese bases, Yamamoto's plane had been shot down. He died on April 18, 1943, just two weeks after his fifty-ninth birthday.

*Goldstein and Dillon, *Pearl Harbor Papers*, p. 132.

handle operations against the British and Americans at the same time. The navy in particular felt strongly that it could either defeat the Americans in a single stroke or at least deliver a stunning blow to their adversary that would give the army a chance to seize the Philippines, Malaya, Hong Kong, and the Dutch East Indies (Indonesia).

Among Americans, few observers rated the Japanese military high enough to worry about. Most people specifically dismissed its chances against a target as well defended and as distant from Japan as Hawaii. Senator Alva Adams of Colorado, for example, doubted seriously that Japan "could bring to [Hawaii] at one time 280 airplanes of a fighting or bombing character."[14] At the other end of the Capitol, House Minority Leader Representative John W. McCormack of Massachusetts stated flatly that "Japan would never move itself against the United States."[15] American newspapers agreed with the politicians in Washington. The *Chicago Tribune*, for example, claimed with supreme confidence that Japan "cannot attack us. That is a military impossibility. Even our base at Hawaii is beyond the effective striking power of her Fleet."[16] The prediction made by Secretary of the Interior Harold Ickes perhaps represented the thinking of the largest share of Americans when it came to likelihood of a Japanese move against Pearl Harbor: "There is going to be no attack on Hawaii. It is too far away."[17]

Faced with what it saw as a threat to Japan's very survival as a regional power, the Imperial cabinet met between September 3 and September 6, 1941, in order to discuss how best to respond to the Americans. The army reiterated its support for an offensive in the southwestern Pacific. The generals proposed multiple coordinated invasions of the American-held Philippines, British Malaya and Hong Kong, and the Dutch East Indies (Indonesia) within days of one another. The Imperial Navy presented its case that a war at sea against the United States was rapidly becoming inevitable and that the land actions planned by the army had to be matched with an attack on Pearl Harbor, perhaps combined with a move against the U.S. bases on Wake Island and the Midway Islands. The assignment of all available troops to the southwest meant that invasions of Hawaii and the Aleutian Islands had to be put on hold. Admiral Chuichi Nagumo warned that conditions favorable to Japanese victory would not last forever: "At the present time we have a chance to win the war, I fear that opportunity will disappear with the passage of time."[18] With the army and navy in agreement and with the Americans refusing to back down, the Konoye cabinet made the decision to continue negotiations but prepare for war. Yamamoto was ordered to begin operational planning and crew training for an attack on Pearl Harbor.

"Things would automatically begin to happen"

The September Imperial conference set the Japanese army and navy to work. The cabinet, however, left open the possibility of a negotiated settlement with the United States. War was much more likely than ever, but many Japanese leaders still hoped for peace. First among them was Emperor Hirohito himself. The emperor was not afraid to lead his subjects into battle, but a clash with the United States would surely become a war for national survival. It was not to be entered into lightly, the emperor thought. There had to be some other way to resolve the dispute with the Americans short of the course advocated by the admirals and generals. "All the seas . . . are as brothers to one another," the emperor wrote in the fall of 1941. "Why then do the winds and waves of strife rage so turbulently throughout the world?"[1]

The seas were, as the emperor described them, turbulent indeed. Even Admiral Kimmel could sense trouble. American planners had long anticipated a strike at Hawaii either opening a war or coming within days of the first shots. The chief of naval operations had already warned the admiral of a weekend attack, as had the Martin-Bellinger Report, and now Kimmel did likewise to his subordinates. If talks with the Japanese broke down, Kimmel told them, the subsequent "declaration of war may be preceded by . . . a surprise attack on ships in Pearl Harbor."[2] He placed specific emphasis on the possibility of an attack *preceding* a declaration of war, an open acknowledgment of the fact that Hawaii could expect little or no warning before Japan struck. Kimmel thus put his men and ships through no fewer than 15 air-raid drills between April and November 1941, each one presuming a dawn attack by carrier-borne planes. The admiral was expecting the worst.

Yamamoto was as well. According to one of his officers, Yamamoto was "quite ready for the worst case."[3] He had been kept up to date on the progress of the negotiations in Washington, D.C., and was well aware that Ambassador Nomura was getting nowhere. Secretary of State Hull was standing firm on the main issues at the heart of the disagreement between Japan and the United States. Before the oil and money could flow again, Hull reiterated, Japan had to withdraw from Indochina and China. Those points were non-negotiable from the American standpoint. The Japanese also refused to budge. The talks were at an impasse.

Yamamoto moved the preparations for Operation Hawaii into high gear. On October 2, commanders of the Japanese air and sea fleets met aboard the aircraft carrier *Akagi*. There, they were told the full details of the plan for a surprise attack on Pearl Harbor. As the officers stood speechless, two scale models were unveiled before them, one of Oahu and another of Pearl Harbor itself. The models had been constructed using

Hirohito, the 124th emperor of Japan, is shown here in a photograph from 1949. Hirohito was born in Tokyo in 1901 and reigned during the Showa era, the longest in Japanese history, from 1926 until his death in 1989. In 1946, he gave up his legendary divinity and most of his powers to become a democratic constitutional monarch.

precise information about the harbor and the location of the ships within it supplied by Japanese agents in Hawaii. In a message intercepted by the United States in September and subsequently deciphered by MAGIC operators (MAGIC was the codename for information gained from deciphering certain Japanese intelligence) but ignored by the military, Tokyo had requested details on how deep Pearl Harbor was, when ships were at anchor there, and the location of each vessel on any given day. Using this information, Yamamoto had nearly exact replicas of his target made to order. "I never thought the plans were anything like this," a senior flight officer remarked to Admiral Yamamoto when he saw the models, "but now that I know what it's all about, I'll give it the best I have!"[4] The others nodded in agreement, and a study session in which the commanders scrutinized the replicas, discussed routes of approach, and debated the best ways to destroy the assigned targets began. They then dispersed to their units to inform their senior pilots of Yamamoto's plan. When the fliers discovered the nature of their next mission, they were ecstatic. "I was born a boy at the right time," one of them shouted.[4]

The decision about the target had been made. The only real question was the best time to strike. Focused as it was on land operations in the southwestern Pacific, the Japanese army favored any date from October to early April for the beginning of hostilities. This was the only window of suitable weather between the region's drenching monsoon seasons. The navy argued for a start date anywhere from late November through the first weeks of December. This tighter timeline was based on Genda's insistence on a northerly route for the Hawaii task force. In order to ensure complete surprise, the Japanese ships would have to maintain radio silence and travel nearly 3,000 miles without encountering any other vessels while sailing through waters that were notoriously storm tossed. The North Pacific was calm enough for large numbers of heavy ships to sail in the sort of tight formation that made radio silence possible only in late November and early December. This fact had been confirmed by the ocean liner *Taiyo Maru*, which sailed across the northern waters in October and later reported to the

Imperial Navy about sea conditions and ship traffic. Looking at the requirements of both military branches, a compromise date was settled on to allow for simultaneous sea and land operations with maximum likelihood of surprising the enemy. Should Nomura fail to come to an agreement with the Americans, war would begin on December 7.

The common sailors and airmen of the Imperial Navy as yet knew nothing of their leaders' scheme. For them, the only inkling that something was about to happen came in the form of intensified training, much of it involving dive bombing and torpedo attacks. The sailors understood that war was likely but none of them dreamed that Pearl Harbor would be the target. "I wonder where the place will be?" many said. "Could it be Singapore or Manila? Guess it couldn't be either of those places because there is no fleet at those places. Surely, it's not Hawaii!" Hawaii, they thought, was too far away, and the water at Pearl Harbor was too shallow for the torpedoes with which they had practiced.

This would have been true had Commander Genda not been working frantically on what he called "the torpedo problem."[6] The standard torpedoes in use in 1941 dove too deeply on water entry for use at depths that matched Pearl Harbor's 40 feet. A torpedo dropped into the water would merely bury itself in the port's muddy bottom. Genda's solution was clever: He ordered the torpedoes used in Operation Hawaii to be fitted with special wooden fins that limited the dive angle. Genda then instructed the torpedo plane pilots to reduce their speed during their attack runs and lower their altitude to put their aircraft closer to the water at the point of release. His novel modifications and tactics worked perfectly. Training could now proceed.

Operation Hawaii seemed to take on a life of its own. Task force *Kido Butai* rapidly came together as a collection of 57 warships and submarines built around a core of 6 state-of-the-art aircraft carriers—the *Akagi, Kaga, Soryu, Hiryu, Zuikaku,* and *Shokaku*. In all, these vessels represented the 1st, 2nd, and 5th Carrier Divisions of the Imperial Navy. They carried within them an assembly of nearly 400 aircraft, including fighters, dive bombers, level bombers, torpedo planes, and seaplanes of models considered by many to be the best in the world. Airplanes such as the Aichi D3A1 Type 99 (Val) dive bomber and the Nakajima B5N1 Type 97 (Kate) torpedo plane were unmatched by anything Japan's enemies could put in the air. These machines would bear the primary responsibility for the attack on Pearl Harbor's warships. The skies above them, however, would be prowled by one of the finest fighter airplanes of World War II, the Mitsubishi A6M2 Type 00 (Zeke). In Operation Hawaii, the A6M2, referred to simply as the Zero, was assigned to clear the skies of enemy interceptors before turning its machine guns on ground targets.

Accompanying the carriers and the air fleet would be a battle group that consisted of 2 battleships, 2 cruisers, 10 destroyers, 7 oil tankers, and 30 submarines, of which 5 were two-man midget submarines designed to slip into Pearl Harbor and support the air attack with precision torpedo strikes. Yamamoto gave command of this awesome force to Admiral Nagumo. After a period of training at Kagoshima Bay, on the island of Kyushu—training that included mock attack runs against a small-scale model of Pearl Harbor—Nagumo ordered the task force to assemble at Hitokappu Bay in the far northern Kurile Islands.

As the navy geared itself for battle, Japan's ambassador worked feverishly to negotiate a peace agreement with the United States. Nomura understood well that he had a strict deadline. In October, the Konoye government fell and the prime minister was replaced by General Hideki Tojo, a man bent on conquest and determined to see Japanese domination of East Asia. No sooner had Tojo taken office than he wired a message to Nomura that was promptly intercepted and decoded by the Americans. The message instructed Nomura to continue his talks, but if no progress were made by November 25, Tojo warned, "things would automatically begin to happen."[7] Nomura could not have known that November 25 was the planned departure date for the Hawaii task force then gathering in the Kuriles, nor could he have imagined that his government had already decided on war if the impasse at the negotiating table were not broken soon. That decision was made on November 5 at a cabinet meeting that included representatives of the army, navy, and civilian government.

Twelve days later, Yamamoto's headquarters issued Combined Fleet General Order No. 1/Task Force Order No. 1 to the ships at Hitokappu Bay: "The Task Force [will sail and] attack the main force of the American Fleet in the Hawaii area and deal it a mortal blow . . . [but] should negotiations with America prove successful, the Task Force is to return at once."[8] Only a breakthrough by Nomura could stop the planned attack on Pearl Harbor now; after December 3, not even detection by American patrol craft could bring Admiral Nagumo's force back home. If discovered then, Nagumo was ordered to fight his way to Hawaii and complete his mission.

Tension filled the air at Hitokappu Bay as Yamamoto visited the task force's flagship, the *Akagi*, on November 17. Though he hoped for peace, the admiral was ready for war and he wanted to speak directly to his men one last time. "Our opponent this time is not an easy one," he warned. "She is of a much higher rating than the enemies Japan has fought until today, and is a much stronger enemy. . . . I'm praying for the best effort from all of you."[9] Privately, Yamamoto confided to a friend, "I fear the military strength of the United States." Should war break out, he continued, "How dangerous the future of the Empire would be."[10] Japan's top admiral knew from the years he had spent in the United States that America possessed vast material resources, almost limitless industrial capacity, and a tenacious will to fight once provoked. Defeating the Americans would be no small task.

As the Japanese put the final touches on Operation Hawaii, diplomats in Washington were trying to work the problem out peacefully. Above, Saburo Kurusu (right), Japan's special envoy, was accompanied by Secretary of State Cordell Hull (center), and Japanese ambassador Kichisaburo Nomura.

As the Japanese put the final touches on Operation Hawaii, the diplomats in Washington worked with renewed vigor toward a solution to the problem they faced. Ambassador Nomura, now joined by Special Envoy Saburo Kurusu, and Secretary of State Hull could sense that their options were running out in terms of finding some way short of war to limit Japanese expansion while at the same time lifting the U.S. embargoes. Hoping to break the deadlock, Nomura and Kurusu submitted something akin to a final offer from the imperial government. The Japanese team had already been told that, if Tokyo reached the end of its patience, a message that indicated an irrevocable war order would be broadcast over short-wave radio to all Japanese embassies located in major countries. The Washington, D.C., embassy was instructed to listen for the code words "Higashi No Kazeame (east wind rain)" during the weather forecast portion of the daily radio news report.[11] Should they receive that message, Nomura and Kurusu were immediately to "destroy all code papers, etc."[12] The envoys understood the instructions perfectly: The destruction of code materials was a prelude to war.

GENERAL SHORT'S WAR WARNING

The November 27 "war warning" sent by Chief of Naval Operations Admiral Harold Stark to Admiral Kimmel was clear and unequivocal: War with Japan was imminent, and Kimmel should prepare for it. The similar message relayed from Army Chief of Staff General George Marshall to the commander of the Hawaiian Department, Lieutenant General Short, was not so straightforward.

Since 1941, debates about the alleged vagueness of Marshall's warning have raged. Many scholars have argued that the chief of staff should have expressed his concerns with greater clarity and emphasis and that Short's confusion over exactly what steps to take to prepare his command for hostilities was totally understandable. Other historians have blamed Short for not reading a plainly worded message carefully enough, thus playing into Japanese hands and setting up his command for disaster on December 7. Readers can judge for themselves whether Short was a victim or a villain after reading the text of General Marshall's message, reprinted in full. (Note: Periods and commas have been inserted where telegraphic form required the actual use of the words *period* and *comma*.)

Nomura and Kurusu delivered Japan's final peace proposals to Hull on November 20. The proposals, entitled Plan A and Plan B, offered alternative short- and long-term deals that would effectively restrict Japanese expansion without requiring any withdrawal from either Indochina or China. Given the fact that the proposals said nothing really new, President Roosevelt accurately concluded that "the Japanese are doing everything they can to stall until they are ready" for military action.[13] While the State Department studied the Japanese

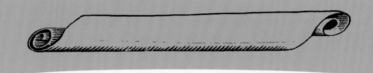

PRIORITY MESSAGE NO. 472 TO COMMANDING GENERAL, HAWAIIAN DEPARTMENT: Negotiations with Japan appear to be terminated to all practical purposes with only the barest possibilities that the Japanese Government might come back and offer to continue. Japanese future action unpredictable but hostile action possible at any moment. If hostilities cannot, repeat cannot, be avoided the United States desires that Japan commit the first overt act. This policy should not, repeat not, be construed as restricting you to a course of action that might jeopardize your defense. Prior to hostile Japanese action you are directed to undertake such reconnaissance and other measures as you deem necessary but these measures should be carried out so as not, repeat not, to alarm civil population or disclose intent. Report measures taken. Should hostilities occur you will carry out the tasks assigned in rainbow five so far as they pertain to Japan. Limit discussion of this highly secret information to minimum essential officers.

Marshall*

*Prange, *Pearl Harbor,* p. 651.

offers, Nagumo's task force made its final preparations to sail for Hawaii. Well-trained and eager for action, the Japanese sailors and airmen practiced relentlessly for the coming operation. Maintenance crews closely examined all the aircraft, and ships' gunners checked their antiaircraft artillery in anticipation of the counterattack by American planes that they all felt certain would follow the raid on Pearl Harbor. Pilots studied maps of Pearl Harbor and silhouettes of the ships they had been assigned to destroy.

Emotions were running high. In an effort to calm his men's nerves, Admiral Nagumo allowed ample time for recreation and exercise. When not on duty, they were even permitted to drink beer and sake (a Japanese wine). Nagumo himself, however, could find no relief from his worrying about the attack. What if his force were detected at sea? What if he were surprised by one of the American aircraft carriers en route? What about all those American submarines that naval intelligence had said were lurking around Hawaii? On top of these concerns, the admiral had to consider issues of fuel and communication. Of his carriers, only the *Kaga*, *Shokaku*, and *Zuikaku* could make it to Hawaii and back on their own fuel supplies. The remaining three carriers would have to pack every available onboard space with oil drums. His battleships and cruisers had the capability to sail roundtrip without tanker assistance, but all of the other vessels in the supporting battle group would have to be refueled at sea. Then there was the problem of holding 57 ships in formation across 3,000 miles of ocean without radio communication and blacked out at night. Considering these difficulties and the dangers inherent in an attack against a powerful enemy, it is not surprising that, on the day his task force sailed, Nagumo asked one of his commanders, "What do you think about the forthcoming operation? . . . I wonder if it will be successful." The officer responded confidently, "Don't worry, sir, . . . I'm sure it will come out well." To this, Nagumo replied somberly, "You're an optimist. . . ."[14]

Cordell Hull was drafting his reply to Plans A and B as Nagumo sailed on November 25. In it, the secretary of state demanded once again that Japan leave China and Indochina as a precondition for further negotiations. "The Government of Japan," Hull wrote on November 26, "will withdraw all military, naval, air and police forces from China and Indochina."[15] Then, and only then, could the two negotiating teams discuss lifting embargoes and unfreezing assets. The Japanese were silent. The next day, Admiral Kimmel received the following message from Admiral Stark in Washington: "This dispatch is to be considered a war warning. Negotiations with Japan looking toward stabilization of conditions in the Pacific have ceased and an aggressive move by Japan is expected within the next few days. . . . Execute an appropriate defensive deployment . . . take appropriate measures against sabotage."[16]

At the same time, General Short received a similar communication from Army Chief of Staff General George Marshall that directed Short "to undertake such reconnaissance and other measures as you deem necessary but the measure should be carried out so as not, repeat not, to alarm civil population or disclose intent."[17] Both Kimmel and Short were further ordered to implement War Plan Rainbow 5—war with Japan.

Climb
Mount Nitaka

The negotiations between Japan and the United States were essentially over, and the Japanese task force had put to sea. Yet despite the November 27 war warnings, neither Admiral Kimmel nor Lieutenant General Short fully understood the messages they had received from Washington. Both assumed that their superiors were concerned primarily with defending Pearl Harbor against something less than a full-scale attack. The first thing that came to Kimmel's and Short's minds was sabotage. Marshall's message, in fact, had specifically mentioned it. Hawaii's commanders thus took steps to keep their ships, planes, and personnel safe from harm inflicted by Japanese agents. Kimmel ordered his ships, at least those not already at sea on exercises or escort duty, to be kept in port, where he could defend them better. The admiral also moved to reinforce the airfields and garrisons on Midway and Wake Islands by dispatching the aircraft carrier USS *Lexington* with planes for Midway and ordering the carrier USS *Enterprise* to prepare to leave no later than December 5 for Wake Island. Short had the army aircraft stationed at Oahu's Hickham, Wheeler, and Bellows airfields put on alert, brought out onto their runways, and lined up wingtip to wingtip. General Short could have placed his fighters in bombproof bunkers to protect against an air strike or dispersed them to smaller outlying airstrips, but he reasoned that bringing them out where they could be better guarded was more suitable to the threat he faced.

Short and Kimmel saw themselves as following both the letter and intent of the war warnings, and they acted to protect the men and equipment under their command. The matter of reconnaissance proved a bit more difficult. The Army Air Corps had light bombers on hand that were capable of monitoring the waters around Oahu, and the Navy had PBY Catalina flying boats designed precisely for long-range reconnaissance. The problem was numbers. Only 69 PBYs were ready for duty, and only a handful of bombers were cleared for flight. When pulled together, then, the patrol units available to Kimmel and Short could effectively search the seas to the south and west of Oahu. That left the northern sectors unwatched. The Army had recognized this deficiency and decided to remedy it by employing an experimental radar system.

In August 1941, the Hawaiian Department received six mobile air search radar sets, each with a functional range of 150 miles. With these, Short's air defense team could monitor the northern approaches and direct interceptors to deal with any enemy coming from that direction. The Opana Station, in particular, could keep a close eye on the exact spot where an attack force emerging from the North Pacific would enter Hawaiian airspace. The combination of bombers, PBYs, and radar reassured Kimmel and Short that they would discover any Japanese task force long before its aircraft posed a danger to Pearl Harbor. Having been advised of the Japanese preference

Major General Walter C. Short, U.S. Army commander, is shown in January 1946. Along with Admiral Husband Kimmel, Short was accused of dereliction of duty in the aftermath of the attack on Pearl Harbor. It was not until May 25, 1999, that the Senate voted 52–47 to exonerate Short and Kimmel.

for early morning attacks, Short took the additional precaution of having his radar stations operate between 4:00 a.m. and 7:00 a.m. After 7:00 a.m., Short figured, the chance of a surprise air raid dropped off to nearly nothing.

While Kimmel and Short prepared to defend their posts, Admiral Nagumo's First Carrier Striking Force was plowing through the fog and waves of the North Pacific, maintaining the strictest radio silence. Ship-to-ship messages were sent via semaphore flags (handheld flags used for signaling) during the day and blinker lamp by night. Radio sets were shut off and their transmitter keys sealed to prevent any accidental tap that might reveal the task force's presence. The nighttime blackout was so complete that not so much as the flame of a cigarette lighter was to be visible above decks. Signal lights were to be employed only if absolutely necessary.

Complete radio silence from six Japanese aircraft carriers concerned American intelligence officers. From November 25 on, no one knew where a sizable part of the Imperial Navy was located. Three carrier divisions seemed to have disappeared. Puzzled, the Americans fell back on the assumption that the ships in question had to be in home waters. Twice before, in February and again in July 1941, the carriers had gone silent, and each time it turned out that they had been at port in Japan. U.S. intelligence knew from MAGIC intercepts that a large number of vessels was steaming southward in the direction of the Philippines and the East Indies, and the carriers were not with them. It was concluded that they were safely at port. In truth, by December 1, the carriers were crossing the International Date Line headed for Pearl Harbor.

As Nagumo's silent fleet slipped ever closer to Hawaii, the Imperial cabinet met once again. Prime Minister Tojo rejoiced, "Now we are going to get involved in a great war."[1] The wheels of Japan's war machine were in motion and picking up speed with each day. On December 1, following the "east wind rain" broadcast, Tokyo wired Nomura and Kurusu in Washington. They were told to "discontinue use of your code machine and dispose of it immediately . . . you will of course burn the machine codes."[2] The next day, the embassy was instructed to stop "at once using your code machine and destroy it completely."[3] Embassies would be given such ominous instructions only in anticipation of a break in diplomatic relations and imminent hostilities. Nomura and Kurusu were left with no doubt. Their country would soon be at war.

Japan's diplomats had their orders, and, on December 2, so did Admiral Nagumo. As his ships headed east, toward the point where they would begin the final southward run to Hawaii, Nagumo received the "go" code from Japan. "Climb Mt. Nitaka," he was commanded, "X day [7th] December."[4] Nagumo ordered his deck and flight officers to prepare the strike teams for the attack on Pearl Harbor. Strangely, the prevailing mood was one of relief. Up to this day, there had always been the slight possibility that a last-minute settlement might be reached, an agreement that would scrub their mission. Now, there was no turning back except in victory or defeat. The letdown of returning home without doing battle would have been unbearable for the pilots who had spent months in training for Operation Hawaii. Their leader, Commander Mitsuo Fuchida, knew this, so he was thrilled to tell his men that the attack was on. Still, he reminded them that there was no time to waste. They had just five days to get ready for the single largest air operation in history, a surprise attack that involved more than 350 combat aircraft.

Back at Pearl Harbor, Kimmel and Short waited and worried. Kimmel especially was frustrated that no one at headquarters in Washington or Hawaii could tell him where the Japanese carriers were at the moment. Quizzing one of his intelligence officers, Kimmel remarked, "Then you don't know where Carrier Division 1 and Carrier Division 2 are?" Commander Edwin Layton replied sheepishly, "No, sir, I don't. I think they are in home waters, but I don't know for sure...." "Do you mean to tell me," Kimmel barked back, "they could be rounding Diamond Head [just outside Pearl Harbor] and you wouldn't know it?"[5] Struggling for a plausible response, Layton claimed that if the Japanese carriers were in Hawaiian waters they would have been found already.

First Carrier Striking Force had not been discovered, however. In fact, the carriers *Shokaku* and *Zuikaku* reported to Nagumo on December 3 that there was "no indication of our

Task Force being detected."[6] Pearl Harbor was unaware that an armada of Japanese warships was already turning southward on its final approach. Japanese intelligence confirmed what Nagumo's sailors and airmen sensed: They had seen no signs of either patrol planes or the American submarines that were said to be on station in the North Pacific. Spies in Hawaii reported that American sailors had been given shore leave as usual. American radio traffic was normal. Everything was going according to plan, except for one thing.

Minoru Genda's original plan had emphasized the absolute necessity of catching the Pacific Fleet's carrier force at Pearl Harbor and destroying it there. Yamamoto's six-month window to operate freely in the Pacific could open only if the *Enterprise*, *Lexington*, and *Saratoga* were in port on the day of the attack. If they were not, America's ability to project power and strike back at Japan would remain intact and the mission to Hawaii would be a strategic failure no matter how many other vessels were destroyed. Nagumo, therefore, was left wondering whether the American carriers would be where they should be on the morning of the attack. As fate would have it, the *Lexington* and *Enterprise* had already put to sea with their consignments of aircraft for Wake and Midway Islands; the *Saratoga* had long since departed for the West Coast, where it was scheduled for routine repairs. For Kimmel, sending the carriers out was no small matter. As of December 5, he still did not know the location of the Japanese carrier divisions. Neither did the *Enterprise*'s skipper, Admiral William Halsey. Before taking his ship out, in fact, he had pointedly asked Kimmel, "What should I do if I run into any Japs?" Kimmel replied, "Bill, use your own common sense." Never one to avoid a fight, Halsey was satisfied. "That's the best damn order I've ever received," he said.[7]

The destruction of the American aircraft carriers lay at the heart of Genda's strategy for Japanese command of the Pacific. Now, not only were they gone, but Nagumo, Genda, and Fuchida had no idea where they were. Nagumo worried incessantly that his fleet had been secretly detected and that the American carriers would be waiting to pounce on him somewhere near Hawaii. Ironically, he knew as much about the American ships as the Americans knew about his; both, in this sense, were entering the upcoming battle at a disadvantage. Which side would ultimately benefit from the confusion was as yet unknown.

COMMANDER MITSUO FUCHIDA
(1902–1976)

Nationalist Pilot

The man at the controls of the lead plane at Pearl Harbor was a devoted Japanese nationalist who never doubted the justness of his emperor's cause. Born in 1902, the Year of the Tiger, Mitsuo Fuchida was a shy child who worked hard in school and enjoyed playing outdoors, especially if the games involved either hunting or mock battles. As a young man, Fuchida set admission to the Japanese Naval Academy at Eta Jima as his goal. He later remembered that the academy appealed to him because "the sea was the native place of my heart." After struggling to pass the physical and written exams, Fuchida was allowed to enter Eta Jima as a midshipman.

During the following years, he studied endlessly and discovered that he had a love of flight. While at the academy, Fuchida was also introduced to Minoru Genda. Flying and Genda set the course for Fuchida's career. During the 1920s and 1930s, Fuchida worked his way up through the ranks of the Imperial Navy and gained a well-deserved reputation as a fine pilot. Given all of his qualities and his connection to Genda, Fuchida was a natural pick to lead the Pearl Harbor mission. Unlike every other pilot who flew on December 7, Fuchida lived to see the end of the war. His suffering was substantial though: He had to lie in bed with appendicitis during the historic

Standing on the *Akagi*'s bridge, Admiral Nagumo scanned the horizon for the American carriers and watched the waves for signs of enemy submarines. The closer his ships got to Hawaii, the more apprehensive he became. Nagumo's pilots, on the other hand, brimmed with relaxed confidence. Commander Fuchida encouraged this mindset. Daily, he strolled the deck of the *Akagi*, looking over its aircraft and reassuring

battle of Midway, and he watched as the air fleet he loved so much was decimated between 1942 and 1945 by the American enemies. After the dropping of the atomic bomb on Hiroshima in August 1945, Fuchida toured the shattered city with other officers, many of them close friends. Afterward, he watched helplessly as every one of them died of either radiation sickness or cancer. Fuchida miraculously remained unharmed.

When his country surrendered the following September, Fuchida stood on the deck of the USS *Missouri* and stoically endured the humiliation of seeing his leaders sign the document that made Japan's defeat official. The hardships of war, the horror of atomic devastation, and the indignity of coming home a defeated warrior combined to encourage a deep spirituality in Fuchida. Although he had never been particularly religious, he converted to Christianity and became an evangelist, spreading the message of Jesus Christ throughout Japan and the United States. In later life, Fuchida came to grips with his role in starting World War II and embraced the land he once attacked. He even became an American citizen in 1967. He then spent the rest of his days enjoying his faith and his wife and two children. After a full and complete life, Fuchida died on May 30, 1976.

his men with easy smiles and bold predictions of victory. If all went as planned, Fuchida was sure that his team could take the Americans by surprise and deal them a blow from which they might not recover.

Nearly 6,000 miles away in Washington, D.C., Secretary of State Hull was waiting impatiently for the Japanese reply to his latest demands for a withdrawal from Indochina and China. While he did so, on December 6, American intelligence intercepted an odd communication from Tokyo to Nomura. The embassy was told to stand by for an important message to be sent in 14 parts. Throughout the night of December 6–7, the parts arrived at the Japanese embassy. Each one was decoded by embassy personnel and retyped, but for security reasons the typing was done by Japanese employees and not by the regular American typists. Unskilled at the keys, the Japanese worked very slowly. Their job was complicated further by Nomura's constant requests for clarification from Tokyo as to the precise wording of the various parts. Finally, in the early morning of December 7, the fourteenth part came in. It was followed at 11:00 a.m. by a precise order. Nomura was to take the entire 14-part message and deliver it to Hull at exactly 1:00 p.m. Washington time, 7:30 a.m. Hawaiian time. When President Roosevelt was briefed on the message he calmly noted, "This means war."[8]

As the night of December 6 became the morning of December 7, the War Department and Navy Department began to stir and the Japanese task force on the seas north of Oahu began final preparations for combat. While mechanics began their final preflight service checks, the submarines that had accompanied the task force went to work. Some of them slipped in and took up picket stations near Oahu to screen and protect the approaching warships. Others scouted the Lahaina anchorage on the island of Maui, a secondary American port that the Navy often used for its vessels. The submarines assigned to this duty were to ensure that no ships had unexpectedly been transferred to Lahaina from Pearl Harbor. Carefully scouting the anchorage, the sub commanders radioed back to Nagumo that the facilities were empty; the American fleet was definitely at Pearl Harbor and nowhere else. Five of the remaining submarines released their cargo of midget subs. These tiny two-man, two-torpedo subs were ordered to penetrate Pearl Harbor's defenses and wait for the main attack to begin in several hours.

The submarines dispatched by Nagumo did their best to remain invisible; after months of drills, alerts, and false sightings of submarines, every American ship in the vicinity would be looking for them. At 3:42 a.m., one of those ships, the minesweeper USS *Condor*, reported that it had spotted what its commander believed to be the wake of a periscope about two miles outside the mouth of Pearl Harbor. Following established procedures, the destroyer USS *Ward* was sent to investigate the report. Finding no sub in the area, the destroyer stood down but remained on patrol. Lieutenant William Outerbridge, the ship's commander, and the *Ward* had not finished their part in the Pearl Harbor drama just yet.

At 5:00 a.m., two of the destroyers escorting the First Carrier Striking Force launched seaplanes for a final round of preattack reconnaissance. Thirty minutes later, Nagumo gave the command for his flight crews to start their engines. As he did, the admiral turned his carriers into the wind and increased their speed to provide sufficient air flow over their decks for takeoff. Recognizing the historic moment, Nagumo hoisted the signal flags that had been run up at the Battle of Tsushima Strait in 1905 by the legendary Admiral Heihachiro Togo. The message sent by the flags read, "The rise and fall of the Empire depend upon this battle; everyone will do his duty with the utmost effect."[9]

As he began to climb into the cockpit of his plane, Fuchida certainly intended to give his all for Japan. He had lived for this day and his role as lead pilot of the first wave of attackers. Straightening his flight suit, Fuchida was about to board when

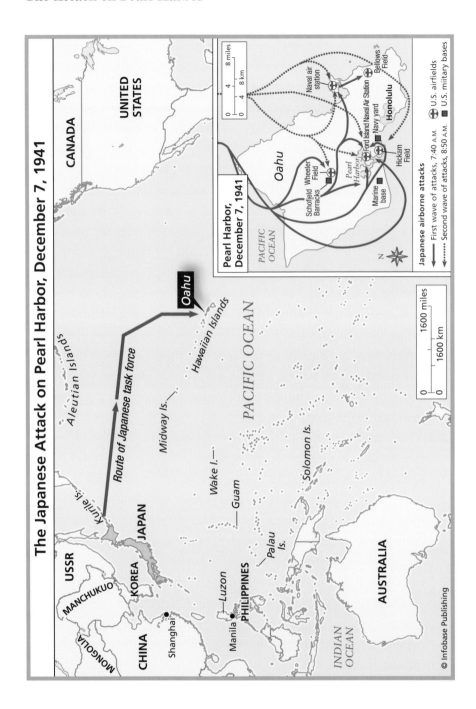

The Japanese Attack on Pearl Harbor, December 7, 1941

© Infobase Publishing

a maintenance crew chief stopped him. Above the whir of pro-pellers and the roar of the wind, the chief smiled and said, "All the maintenance crew would like to go along to Pearl Harbor. Since we can't we want you to take this *hachimaki* as a symbol we are with you in spirit."[10] Fuchida smiled and looked down at a headband that bore good tidings written on either side of a rising sun. The commander lifted it to his forehead and tied it around his flight cap in the fashion of Japan's ancient warriors, the samurai. Like his ancestors before him, Fuchida was ready to fight and perhaps die for his emperor.

At precisely 6:10 a.m., on December 7, heaving up and down on ocean swells that reached 40 feet in height, the *Akagi, Kaga, Soryu, Hiryu, Shokaku,* and *Zuikaku* launched their air-craft into a sky just beginning to reveal a hint of dawn on the horizon. Plane after plane taxied into position and then thun-dered across the flight deck before rising into the air. Weighed down with their loads of bombs and torpedoes, the Kates and Vals dipped slightly after leaving the deck and then climbed together in two great circles, one rotating clockwise and the other counterclockwise. This way, all of the planes could come together and speed toward their target as one massive aerial force.

The nimble Zero fighters took off last and raced skyward to their position above the others. By 6:20 a.m., the first wave was airborne. Arranging themselves into a three-tiered formation,

(opposite page) **This map shows the route of the Japanese attack on Pearl Harbor. On November 26, 1941, six carriers, two battleships, three cruisers, and nine destroyers left the Kurile Islands and sailed east toward the Hawaiian Islands. On the night of December 6, the Japanese had reached their targeted position and launched a full-scale attack on Pearl Harbor early the next morning.**

Fuchida's 183 first-wave aircraft headed for Pearl Harbor. As they flew southward, the sun began to rise, casting sunbeams that made the entire picture look just like Imperial Japan's battle flag. Fuchida saw this and grinned, motioning to the other planes to take a look at what he considered a good omen. At that same moment, the Japanese planes picked up the commercial radio signal from Honolulu. Surprised to find the station on the air so early on a Sunday morning, the pilots laughed. They laughed harder when it turned out that the station was playing a Japanese song.

Fuchida's men were listening to light music as their comrades in the second wave were lifting off the decks of the Japanese carriers. Less than an hour after the first wave had departed, 167 bombers and fighters followed them into the sky. None of these airplanes carried torpedoes because the element of surprise would be lost after the initial attack. Slow and low-flying, torpedo planes would never survive the withering antiaircraft fire that the second formation would surely meet. With that, 350 planes had been put in the air in a mere 90 minutes. Nagumo was rightfully proud of his sailors and aircrews. Two waves of aircraft were headed toward Pearl Harbor, and submarines were either on station or already slipping into Pearl Harbor. There was nothing left to do but wait. In just under another hour, Fuchida and the lead group would commence their attack, and success or failure would be the result. All this time, Pearl Harbor slept.

Sunday Morning

As the Japanese attack planes raced toward their target, the embassy in Washington, D.C., continued to decode, translate, and type the 14-part message from Tokyo. American intelligence officers, already alerted to the significance of the final installment, notified the appropriate military and civilian leaders that a break in diplomatic relations and perhaps a declaration of war were imminent. Colonel Rufus Bratton took the job of informing Army Chief of Staff General Marshall about the message and its implications. Marshall had been told previously that the Japanese were destroying their codes, and he knew that war was possible at any moment. Inexplicably, however, the general was not in his office on the morning of December 7. Bratton arrived prepared to update Marshall only to find that the chief of staff had not altered his routine; as on every Sunday morning, he was told, Marshall was horseback riding. Bratton waited patiently until the general arrived at 11:25 a.m. It was just after 6:00 a.m. in Hawaii.

When finally briefed on the latest communication between Japan and its embassy, Marshall immediately sensed the significance of the mysterious fourteenth part. He sent an urgent message to General Short on Oahu. The warning went from Marshall's office directly to the Army Signal Center, but the center was experiencing technical difficulties at the time. The officer on duty there took it upon himself to send the cable by Western Union to San Francisco, where it would be relayed by the RCA civilian wire service to its final destination. It did not seem all that important to the Army Signal Center that Marshall's war warning would arrive in Hawaii no earlier than 11:45 a.m. local time. It would get to General Short safely, and that was all that mattered.

While Washington was coming to grips with the likelihood of war, Fuchida and the First Air Fleet flew toward Pearl Harbor. With each mile, Fuchida expected to be discovered and engaged by American air defenses. His fighter escorts searched the horizon for the waves of American interceptors that were certain to show up shortly, but none appeared.

For the midget subs, moving stealthily through the waters outside Pearl Harbor, it was a different story. The scout sighted in the morning darkness by the *Condor* had been able to slip away; another one, spotted by the supply ship *Antares*, was not as lucky. At 6:30 a.m., the *Antares* radioed the *Ward* to report possible hostile contact. A lookout on the *Antares* thought he had seen a conning tower (the observation port mounted above a submarine's deck) cutting through the water. The *Ward*, still on patrol, sped to the sight and arrived in time to catch a glimpse of a submarine attempting to sneak into Pearl Harbor through the port's antisubmarine gates, which were scheduled to be left open until 8:40 a.m. for the *Condor* and another minesweeper. Lieutenant Outerbridge quickly ordered his forward gun turrets to fire on the sub. The destroyer's gunners hit their target easily, forcing it to make an emergency dive. The *Ward* swung around, positioned itself above its wounded prey, and dropped a spread of depth charges. A Navy PBY Catalina flying nearby joined the attack, releasing several bombs over the Japanese intruder. A slowly spreading oil slick after the explosions told the Americans that the Japanese sub had reached the end of its mission.

Having sunk his first ship, Lieutenant Outerbridge excitedly radioed Pearl Harbor that his destroyer had "attacked, fired upon, and dropped depth charges upon submarine operating in defensive sea area."[1] The Catalina pilot did likewise, notifying his superiors that he had "sunk an enemy submarine one mile south of Pearl Harbor."[2] Strangely, neither report generated much interest back at Pearl Harbor. Reports of submarines, all cases of mistaken identification by nervous young officers, were common of late. The *Ward*'s claims would have to be confirmed before anyone would pay much attention.

Meanwhile, Oahu's radar operators were wrapping up another uneventful four-hour shift of staring at blank screens. Bored and hungry for breakfast, the men began to turn off their equipment. One by one, the six installations shut down for the day. The mobile set at Opana was scheduled to go dark at 7:00 a.m., but, as the two operators began to flip switches, something caught their eyes. A large blip appeared on their screen. A systems check indicated that the set was functioning properly and within normal limits. There was no mistake: The blip was a flight of at least 50 planes heading toward Oahu from the north at a constant speed. Following standard procedures, the men telephoned the Aircraft Warning Service at Fort Shafter and reported what they were seeing. The officer on duty at the center took the call but assumed that the Opana radar had picked up a flight of B-17 bombers coming in from the mainland. The radar crew was told not to worry and proceed with the scheduled shut down. They reluctantly complied with the orders and switched off at 7:39 a.m. The incoming Japanese planes had no idea that they had been detected. They were now only 20 miles from Pearl Harbor.

As the first wave of Japanese attackers neared Oahu, its pilots redoubled their visual searches for American aircraft. Fuchida thoroughly expected to find at least some defenders to greet him, but, as he drew closer to Pearl Harbor, the skies remained empty. Surprise, Fuchida suspected, had been achieved. As the Japanese planes climbed over Oahu's forest-covered mountains, Fuchida still saw nothing. With the target within range and no enemy activity, he readied his flare gun. According to the attack plan, Fuchida had told his pilots that he would open the canopy of his cockpit and fire a single flare if the flight had gained complete surprise. This would signal the Kate torpedo planes, led by Lieutenant Commander Shigeharu Murata, to swoop in and begin the raid. If, as could still happen, interceptors appeared, indicating that Pearl Harbor was alerted, Fuchida would fire two flares and the dive bombers would take the lead. The Japanese figured that, if Pearl Harbor were on guard against attack, a torpedo run would do no good. The ships at anchor would surely be surrounded by torpedo nets, a protective blanket of steel mesh that could stop underwater weapons. Dive bombers would then have to do the job.

As it turned out, Fuchida approached a Pearl Harbor that was completely unaware of what was in store for it. Emerging from the clouds, the Japanese soon had the anchorage in sight. There was no fighter reception waiting, no torpedo nets, and, better still, almost every ship of the Pacific Fleet was exactly where it should be. Shocked at his good luck, Fuchida thought to himself how much the scene below resembled the scale models he had studied before leaving Japan. Total surprise now confirmed, the Japanese commander slid back the canopy of his plane and fired one flare into the sky. Looking up at the Zero fighters high above the strike wave, Fuchida noticed no change in their flight pattern. If they had seen his flare, they should have peeled off to begin strafing ground targets: In this case, they were not needed for aerial combat.

Frustrated, Fuchida concluded that the attack team had not seen his first flare, so he fired another. As luck would have it, the fighters and the other planes had indeed seen the first signal rocket. Now, seeing another streak skyward, they thought Fuchida wanted the dive bombers to start the attack. Thus, as ordered, the Vals dove down toward the American ships. Fuchida was furious at the mix-up, but he quickly realized that it made little difference given the fact of surprise. Everywhere, Japanese planes shifted to get into attack formation. As they did so, Fuchida's radioman sent out the order for all planes to go in—"To, To, To."[3] The lead plane then broadcast back to Nagumo's carriers and to Admiral Yamamoto, sitting on his flagship, *Nagato*, safely at anchor in Japan, the coded message to indicate success at taking the Americans by surprise: "Tora, Tora, Tora" ("Tiger, Tiger, Tiger").[4]

At 7:55 a.m., Murata's torpedo planes came in low and dropped their weapons. Watching as the slim shapes sped forward, Murata radioed Nagumo, "I have attacked the enemy main force...."[5] Seconds later, nearly simultaneously, explosions ripped through the battleships *Nevada*, *Oklahoma*, *California*, and *West Virginia*. In another moment, the *Utah* erupted into flames and rolled over in its berth.

Aboard the Japanese carriers at sea, the news of the raid was greeted with joy that bordered on ecstasy. One Japanese officer wrote in his diary that, after hearing Fuchida's triumphant message, "All members [of the crew] became wild with joy."[6] Another sailor recalled that "wild joy burst out with the news of 'Tora, Tora ...,'" and added, "Oh, how powerful is the Imperial Navy."[7] Admiral Nagumo was happy to hear of Fuchida's success, and he was relieved that the Americans had put up no initial resistance. The operation had just begun, however, and the admiral worried that all of his planes might not make it back to their carriers safely. The return trip would not be easy, especially for any aircraft that had sustained battle damage over the target. The plan was for the First Carrier Striking Force to launch its airplanes as close as possible to Hawaii and then turn and immediately begin to steam away. On the return leg, the pilots would expend the fuel saved by the close takeoff. This "one short, one long leg" strategy minimized the chances of a successful American counterattack against the Japanese carriers because it would force the enemy to fly ever-extending distances out to the ships and back to base. Attacking a target that was moving away would almost guarantee that any American planes that made it out to the task force would subsequently run out of fuel on the way home and crash into the Pacific.

The planning of Operation Hawaii effectively neutralized an American response by land-based aircraft even before it was made. Still, without knowing the whereabouts of the *Enterprise* and the *Lexington*, Nagumo could not let down his guard. Submarines lurked all around him, as well, and by now they would be alerted to the presence of the Japanese battle group. Pacing the bridge of the *Akagi*, Admiral Nagumo would join in celebrating the air fleet's accomplishment only when all of his planes and pilots were back on board and he was under full power toward Japan.

Back at Pearl Harbor, the devastation continued. Torpedo planes raced here and there, skimming the surface of the water as dive bombers screamed downward toward the American fleet. Everywhere, ships seemed to be exploding. Smoke billowed upward as oil spilled from ruptured fuel tanks into the harbor and caught fire. Hit by two torpedoes dropped by airplanes and at least one fired by a midget sub, the *California* was rocked by explosions and began to roll over. The ship was prevented from capsizing completely only by prompt counterflooding of undamaged compartments. The *Oklahoma*, ravaged by three direct torpedo hits, flooded so quickly that its crew could not duplicate the *California*'s feat. The *Oklahoma* turned upside

Above, the USS *West Virginia* is shown aflame during the attack on Pearl Harbor. Disregarding the dangerous possibility of explosions, sailors manned their boats at the side of the burning battleship to better fight the flames started by Japanese torpedoes and bombs.

down. At 8:10 a.m., the doomed *Arizona* virtually disintegrated after a series of massive explosions. The *Nevada*, hit by one torpedo and several bombs, should have followed the *Arizona* to the bottom, but somehow it managed not only to stay afloat but also to remain capable of movement. Its captain decided to accept the gift fortune had given him and make a run for the open sea. He ordered his engine room to make speed, and, with jets of water shooting up from detonations all around him, the captain frantically backed his ship out of its berth.

Now the reports from the first attack wave poured in. Nagumo's radios hummed: "Torpedoed enemy battleship. Serious damage inflicted. . . . Bombed enemy battleships. Position, Pearl Harbor. . . . Torpedoed enemy heavy cruiser with serious damage inflicted. . . ."[8]

Mixed with these cries of victory were incoming reports from the aircraft assigned to attack Oahu's many airfields. Army airbases at Hickam, Bellows, and Wheeler airfields were struck by a combination of fighters and bombers. The naval air stations at Ford Island and Kaneohe were hit just as hard, and the Marine Corps air station at Ewa was ravaged by Japanese fighters. Japanese planes bombed and strafed undefended runways that were crammed with aircraft lined up wingtip to wingtip, just as General Short had specified. Most of the American planes exploded into flame right where they sat. The few that tried to get airborne were destroyed before a single wheel left the ground. At Ford Island, Navy PBYs were methodically shredded by bombs and machine gun fire. With aircraft and buildings on fire across the airfield, the radio at Ford Island crackled out an alarm for those who still had any doubt in their minds—"Air Raid Pearl Harbor. This is not a drill."[9]

Even with the roar of battle shattering the Sunday morning stillness, for many of the soldiers and sailors, the awful reality of what was happening had not taken hold. At Wheeler Field, the post commander, General Harold Davidson, ran from his house at the sound of the airplane engines and explosions outside. Fuming with anger at what he thought were reckless U.S. Navy exercises, Davidson screamed at an aide, "Can you get the number of any of those planes?"[10] The stunned junior officer looked carefully at the aircraft for American markings and then yelled back, "Christ, General, they've got rising suns painted on them."[11] A sergeant at Hickam Field also mistook the Japanese attackers for U.S. Navy planes until a friend corrected him. Hoping to see the incoming B-17s everyone had been told about, the soldier remarked, "Hey, those are not B-17s, those

This is an aerial view (taken by a Japanese pilot during the attack) of the burning U.S. Hawaiian Air Base at Wheeler Airfield. The Japanese plan involved not only targeting the American ships at Pearl Harbor, but also U.S. aircraft at the airfields nearby.

are Navy planes."[12] "Yes," his friend replied, his voice growing in intensity, "they're navy planes alright, but they're the wrong blasted navy."[13]

The B-17s did arrive at Hickam that morning, in the middle of a ferocious battle. Not expecting to fly into a war, the bombers were low on fuel and had no weapons on board. Jumped by Zeros almost instantly, 11 B-17s miraculously set down in the midst of the destruction, although only 10 did so on what remained of the airfield's runways. One of the planes missed the base altogether and landed on a nearby golf course. In total, three B-17s were damaged and one destroyed.

On the other side of Oahu, at Kaneohe Naval Air Station, Japanese attack planes barreled in and swiftly obliterated half of the PBY Catalinas there. At Ewa, Zeros and Vals combined to execute a merciless assault on the Marine aircraft, support buildings, and barracks. Japanese planes that attacked Wheeler Airfield swept in so low on their bomb runs that Japanese mechanics later found telephone wires wrapped around their landing gear. Like the B-17s at Hickam, a flight of 18 Navy Dauntless dive bombers stumbled into the fight at Ford Island and tried to land. In the confusion, American antiaircraft gunners mistook the planes for the enemy and opened fire. One was shot down; Japanese Zeros got the rest.

Aboard the ships blazing at Pearl Harbor, rescue efforts and frantic attempts to put out fires had begun and the first signs of counterattack had appeared. Where and when they could, sailors grabbed rifles, machine guns, and antiaircraft cannons and returned gunfire. The valor of men such as Dorie Miller, a black mess attendant (a cook and waiter for the ship's dining hall) with no weapons training, was astonishing. Struggling to the deck of the *West Virginia*, Miller put himself behind a gun and began to shoot at Japanese planes, hitting one of the few that went down on December 7. Awarded the Navy Cross for bravery, Miller is remembered as a hero whose example of courage later served to justify the desegregation of the United States armed forces.

As the battle on Oahu raged, Ambassador Nomura went to meet Secretary of State Hull, carrying the 14-part message. It was 12:30 p.m. before Nomura and Kurusu had the final portion fully decoded, translated, and typed. Looking at the clock, Nomura remembered that his instructions were to deliver the message to the Americans at precisely 1:00 p.m. The reason, unknown to Nomura, was simple. Japan, Admiral Yamamoto in particular, wanted to sever relations with the United States 30 minutes before the first bombs fell at Pearl Harbor. This

Third class shipman Dorie Miller (above), a mess attendant on the _West Virginia_, was decorated for firing at Japanese aircraft on his own initiative during the attack on Pearl Harbor. He rescued wounded men and shot down four enemy aircraft.

would avoid the charge of attacking a country with which Japan was still actively negotiating. Failing to do so would make any operation a "sneak" attack rather than a "surprise" attack, a subtle but important difference in international relations. Not informed of Operation Hawaii, Nomura had no idea that the timing of his delivery was so crucial. By the time the Japanese diplomats finally met with Hull at 2:20 p.m., the United States and Japan were already at war. Unlike Nomura, Hull knew this when he read that the "Japanese Government regrets to have to notify the American Government that in view of the attitude of the American Government it cannot but

THE JAPANESE VIEW OF PEARL HARBOR

American voices from December 7 are often heard. The words of politicians, average citizens, and the men who were at Pearl Harbor that day have resonated through American history since 1941. The thoughts and feelings of the men in the First Carrier Striking Force, however, are far less familiar. Their concerns, fears, and hopes are overlooked or, worse, dismissed. The Japanese sailors and airmen, as a result, are stereotyped as heartless aggressors, simply the enemy "other." Yet these men sensed the significance of raid on Pearl Harbor and felt their own unique emotions as the attack began and ended. Here, in the recollections of Vice Admiral Ryunosuke Kusaka, who stood next to Admiral Nagumo throughout the battle, is a glimpse of how the Japanese perceived the events of December 7. This excerpt from Kusaka's memoir records the atmosphere on the *Akagi* just as the attack on the Pacific Fleet was beginning.

As I sat in front of the maps in the operations room [of the *Akagi*] expecting to hear reconnaissance reports from the [destroyer] Tone's and Chikuma's seaplanes which had been dispatched about thirty minutes before, the first report from the Chikuma's plane came in. It read: "The enemy fleet is not in Lahaina consider that it is impossible to reach an agreement through further negotiations."[14] The remainder of the memorandum comprised a withering criticism of American interests and objectives. Hull boiled with anger. "In all my fifty years of public service," the secretary of state seethed, "I have never seen a document that was more crowded with infamous falsehoods and distortions . . . on a scale so large that I never imagined until this day that any Government on this planet was capable

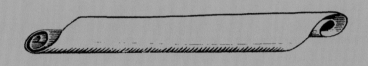

anchorage . . . the enemy fleet is in Pearl Harbor." How pleased we were to receive this report! Instinctively Admiral Nagumo and all of his staff officers looked at each other and could not suppress their smiles. The only thing remaining was to await the result of the attack. A pre-arranged word "Tora," the very word which all attention—not only the Task Force but also the Malaya Invasion Force, the Philippine Force to the south, [Yamamoto's] flagship in Hiroshima Bay and the Imperial General Staff in Tokyo—were focused to catch. Soon a telegram sent from the dive bomber leader to his planes . . . was intercepted. It was soon followed by a telegram order from [Fuchida's] plane notifying all planes "to launch attacks." Sensing that they were now going to launch an attack at last, everyone in the operations room held their breath . . . the long-awaited "tora" was received. At that moment, I was on the bridge with Admiral Nagumo directing action of the force after launching all planes, and could not suppress tears coming down my checks. Without any words, I firmly grasped Admiral Nagumo's hand.*

*Goldstein and Dillon, *Pearl Harbor Papers,* p. 160.

of uttering them."[15] Shaken, Nomura and Kurusu stood to leave; they waited for the usual courtesies but Hull looked away and refused to shake their hands. Only later did Nomura find out why.

Back in Hawaii, by the time Admiral Kimmel made his way to his office overlooking Pearl Harbor, his fleet was in ruins. The Japanese pilots had done their job well. Ships had been transformed into infernos, twisted wrecks, and sinking hulks by the time the second wave of attackers appeared over Oahu at 8:54 a.m. Hoping to put the finishing touch on a historic military victory, the follow-up group of bombers and fighters swooped in. Their comrades in the first wave had met some resistance from a surprised adversary. Four planes had been shot down; another 46 had been damaged. The second wave, however, flew into a different battle, one in which the enemy was armed and ready. Ordered to hit the ships and airfields already struck as well as targets of opportunity, the second attack group's mission was complicated by the successes of the first. Dense smoke obscured many of the objectives. Worse still, Pearl Harbor's antiaircraft batteries were now fully operational and a number of American fighters had managed to get airborne. Five American P-40s took off from the rugged airstrip at Haleiwa, which had been overlooked by the Japanese. The pilots of these planes scored six kills against the second wave. Five more interceptors struggled aloft from the wreckage of Wheeler Airfield. These aircraft shot down an additional two Japanese planes. It was after these aerial battles that the only ground action of the day took place. With help from a Japanese citizen living in Honolulu and a Japanese-American, a downed Japanese pilot broke into several homes and took the occupants hostage before being killed by American troops.

The second wave of Japanese planes accomplished less than the first and suffered more. Many of its bombs missed their marks, and several choice targets escaped because of the cloud of smoke spreading across Pearl Harbor and the antiaircraft fire now being thrown up by the American defenders. In the smoky confusion, the battleship *Nevada* was perhaps the most valuable prize to elude the second wave. Sighted as it was attempting to leave the harbor, the *Nevada* was hammered by repeated bomb drops. The second group of Japanese pilots knew that, if they could sink such an immense vessel in the mouth of the shipping channel, the resulting obstruction would make Pearl Harbor unusable for months. The *Nevada*'s captain had originally planned simply to save his ship, but the obvious and intense Japanese interest in sinking it made him realize that, if the *Nevada* had to go down, it could not be at the entrance to the harbor. Deftly maneuvering the wounded, lumbering ship into shallow water, the captain managed to beach the *Nevada*, thus getting it out of the way. Nonetheless, the Japanese put several more bombs down on top of the now stationary ship.

The Japanese midget subs, like the second wave of airplanes, endured a harrowing morning, one from which not a single boat would return. The primary submarine group that accompanied the Japanese task force spent December 7 scouting, screening, and standing by to rescue any pilots downed in the Pacific. The five midget subs released from it, however, had been given combat assignments inside Pearl Harbor. This meant first penetrating the facility at very shallow depths, firing two torpedoes each while barely submerged, and finally slipping back out to sea undiscovered through the alerted American defenses. Given the dangers of such a mission, it is not surprising that all five subs were lost. The *Ward* sank one at 6:45 a.m. and dropped depth charges on another about half an hour later. One other sub was sent to the bottom of the sea by the destroyer *Monahan* just before the second wave appeared over Oahu. A fourth midget was sighted off the western shores of the island and promptly set upon by an American ship. Damaged and frantically trying to outrun its pursuers, the sub ran aground. Its two crewmen escaped, but one was killed and the other captured, becoming the first Japanese prisoner of war taken by the Americans during World War II. The stranded sub was later floated off the reef it became stuck on, taken to Honolulu, and put on public display. Nothing was ever heard from the fifth submarine after it briefly made radio contact late in the afternoon.

While the subs were struggling to carry out their dangerous assignments, the Japanese pilots high above them were flying through a hail of bullets and pounding away at any available American target. Airfields, barracks, repair shops, offices, anything and everything that could be found was struck hard. Watching the carnage, Admiral Kimmel knew that he would have to answer for the disaster unfolding before him. At one point, a spent bullet shattered his office window and hit the admiral in the chest. Its energy gone, the round did no physical harm. Looking at it Kimmel lamented, "It would have been more merciful if it would have killed me."[16]

By 10:00 a.m., Oahu's military installations were in ruins. Four battleships at Pearl Harbor had been sunk and another four severely damaged. Three destroyers, three light cruisers, one seaplane tender, and four other assorted vessels had also been sent to the harbor's muddy bottom by the Japanese. Total aircraft losses stood at 188 destroyed and 63 damaged. The airfields also suffered extensive damage to runways, hangars, and maintenance buildings. Human casualties amounted to 2,335 dead and 1,143 missing or wounded; many of the wounded carried hideous burn injuries received on the decks of flaming ships. Of the American dead, 2,008 were sailors.

Secure in their total success, the second wave of Japanese airplanes sped away toward Nagumo's carriers. In nearly two hours of solid fighting, the First Air Fleet had a mere 29 aircraft shot down and 70 planes damaged, most very lightly. The navy's only nonairborne material losses were the five midget submarines. Less than 100 Japanese personnel died in the attack. Yamamoto's foresight, Genda's brilliance, and Fuchida's martial prowess had given the empire its greatest victory. One hour and

45 minutes after the planes had left Hawaiian skies, in a final moment of irony, General Marshall's message, warning General Short of the imminent outbreak of war with Japan, arrived at the Army's Oahu headquarters. It was delivered by a young messenger, who just happened to be Japanese American.

The public on the mainland received news of the attack on Pearl Harbor with shocked disbelief. Few were prepared to tune into their favorite Sunday morning shows only to hear, "We are interrupting this program with a special report. At this very moment Japanese airplanes are attacking the United States Naval Base at Pearl Harbor. . . . Stay tuned to this program for further developments."[17] The American people knew that relations between Japan and the United States had been deteriorating in the fall of 1941, but no one imagined that the Japanese possessed either the skill or the audacity to sail nearly 3,000 miles and launch a surprise attack on America's premier Pacific outpost. Before December 7, most Americans were confident that the United States could avoid being dragged into the war that was slowly spreading throughout Europe, Asia, and the Middle East. As the Charleston (West Virginia) *Gazette* put it, only days after the Japanese raid, Americans "honestly thought we could build a wall of steel around ourselves and retire within it in complete safety, there to remain isolated until the storm [of war] passed."[18] Pearl Harbor quashed those hopes forever.

The Aftermath
and Legacy
of Pearl Harbor

The USS *Indianapolis* was returning to Pearl Harbor from patrol duty shortly after the Japanese second wave had departed when one of its crewmen noticed something odd. Surveying the fleet through his binoculars, he turned to his friend and said, "Christ, those silhouettes are all cockeyed."[1] Vessels that should have been sitting proudly upright slumped and leaned this way and that. Some seemed to have half-disappeared in the water, and others were virtually unrecognizable. Smoke still hung in the air. The United States Pacific Fleet had been shattered.

Aboard the Japanese ships of the First Carrier Striking Force, in contrast, laughter and congratulations abounded. Admiral Nagumo's men and planes had savaged America's most important Pacific naval base and escaped without pursuit. To be sure, some surviving PBYs had been launched in a forlorn attempt to hunt down the task force. Between 9:30 a.m. and 3:30 p.m., in fact, 48 search missions had been flown, but none caught up with the carriers as they sped toward Japan. The Japanese slipped away from Pearl Harbor so cleanly that the commander of the destroyer *Akigumo* exclaimed, "I couldn't see one plane of the enemy's counterattack.... How simple war really is!"[2] Nagumo was also pleasantly surprised at the textbook execution of Operation Hawaii. Of course, he and his officers, chief among them Genda and Fuchida, were disappointed that the American carriers had not been in port at the time of the attack, but the Imperial Navy could deal with them later. For now, Nagumo joined his men in celebration, but he reminded them that "there remains a long way to go"[3] and that many battles against the Americans lay ahead.

At home in Japan, the mood was jubilant. When news of the victory was broadcast to the Japanese public, the people reacted with a mixture of absolute joy and national pride. Yet Admiral Yamamoto, Operation Hawaii's architect, the man who imagined and executed it from start to finish, sat quietly as his staff savored the triumph. The commander of the Combined Fleet sensed trouble. The Pearl Harbor raid had taken place before a formal declaration of war had been issued to the United States. That meant that his daring "surprise" attack would be viewed by the Americans as a dastardly "sneak" attack. His new opponents would seek revenge for such deceit. From his years in the United States, Yamamoto knew that nothing angered Americans more than deception, and they would certainly see this operation as an example of such trickery. "Gentlemen," he told his officers, "I'm afraid all we have done is awaken a sleeping giant and filled him with a terrible resolve."[4]

After December 7, Americans were indeed filled with a terrible resolve and a fierce determination to make good on the losses suffered that day. Achieving this end began with the issuing of the sort of formal declaration of war that Japan had denied to the United States prior to Pearl Harbor. The day after

U.S. President Franklin D. Roosevelt appears before a joint session of Congress appealing for a declaration of war against Japan in Washington, D.C. on December 8, 1941.

the Pacific Fleet was smashed, President Roosevelt addressed Congress:

> Yesterday, December 7, 1941—a date which will live in infamy—the United States of America was suddenly and deliberately attacked by the naval and air forces of the Empire of Japan. . . . Hostilities exist. There is no blinking at the fact that our people, our territory, and our interests are in grave danger. With confidence in our armed forces—with the unbounded determination of our people—we will gain the inevitable triumph—so help us God.[5]

Roosevelt asked for and received a declaration of war against Japan, and the United States officially entered World War II.

As the president spoke, the military command at Pearl Harbor moved to assess the damage wrought by the Japanese. The first job was recovery, a process that began even as the acrid smell of smoke still permeated the air and oil-soaked debris littered the water. The shallow depth of Pearl Harbor that had originally confounded Genda as he puzzled over how to use his torpedoes in the attack became a bit of serendipity for the U.S. Navy. Genda had to modify the torpedoes used by the first wave because Pearl Harbor averaged only 40 feet in depth; this fact meant that all but two of the ships sunk by the Japanese planes could be raised and refloated. The *Utah* was already obsolete at the time of the attack and was not worth the effort; the *Arizona* was too far gone. Every other vessel, however, rested in water that allowed divers and repair parties easy access. Although completely capsized, the *Oklahoma*, for example, was righted with little effort. The teams at Pearl Harbor were unable to repair it, though, so the ship stayed at Hawaii until 1947. In a fitting conclusion to the *Oklahoma*'s story, the ship was being towed to the West Coast to be cut up and sold for scrap when the tow cable snapped in a storm. Consigned to the junkyard, the *Oklahoma*, seemingly in protest of its fate, sank fully intact in the open ocean.

Similar and ultimately more successful stories characterized the remainder of the recovery. Yamamoto had told Genda that he needed the American fleet out of his way for six months. The battleship *Nevada*, however, was refloated in February 1942, the *California* in March, and the *West Virginia* in May. The *Maryland, Tennessee,* and *Pennsylvania*, all damaged in the attack, were back in service by early spring. Even the destroyer *Shaw*, centerpiece of the famous photo that shows the vessel exploding in flame as its bow is blown off by a Japanese bomb, was able to sail to San Francisco under its own power in February 1942. The *Shaw* took part in the Battle

Above, the Navy rights the capsized USS *Oklahoma*. The teams at Pearl Harbor were unable to repair it, though, so the ship stayed at Hawaii until 1947. While it was being towed to the West Coast to be cut up and sold for scrap, the tow cable snapped in a storm and the ship sank fully intact in the open ocean.

of Santa Cruz that October, less than a year after Pearl Harbor. By 1944, in short, the Pacific Fleet, decimated in Operation Hawaii, had been totally restored and had become part of a massive new Navy that consisted of 104 aircraft carriers of various types, 8 additional fully modern battleships, 46 heavy and light cruisers, 349 destroyers, 420 destroyer escorts, 75 frigates, and 203 submarines. The Japanese victory proved short-lived indeed.

The fleet at Pearl Harbor had benefited not only from the port's shallow water but also from the Japanese decision not to destroy the oil storage and maritime repair facilities located there. The order to leave the latter two areas unharmed was made by Admiral Nagumo himself, based on his calculation of the dangers inherent in lingering too long in Hawaiian waters. Nagumo's fuel supply for his ships and planes was uncertain, and he had solid information that indicated that American submarines were nearby. Most troubling was the inability to pinpoint the location of the carriers *Enterprise* and *Lexington*. With these ships and their aircraft wandering around somewhere unknown, Nagumo felt that he had to depart for home after the second wave had safely returned. Although some of his officers advocated a third wave, the admiral said no. His ships were vulnerable to counterattack, and most of the third-wave planes would have run out of fuel on the flight back to the task force. True, destruction of the oil and repair depots would have been a serious strategic blow to the United States, ending the hopes that an American fleet could stop the Japanese land campaign that began in the Southwestern Pacific the same day as Pearl Harbor. Loitering around Hawaii was simply too dangerous, however, and Nagumo sailed for Japan. He arrived to cheering crowds on December 23.

As it turned out, leaving Pearl Harbor capable of supporting operations was a fatal mistake. Without a functioning Pacific base, missions such as the Doolittle Raid, an air strike against Tokyo by B-25 bombers flown from the deck of the aircraft carrier *Hornet* in April 1942, would have not have been considered, let alone carried out. Major naval engagements such as the Battle of the Coral Sea, a battle in which the U.S. Navy succeeded in preventing Japan from cutting the sea lanes to Australia and launching air raids against it, would not have taken place. Far from being erased as a factor in the American war effort, Pearl Harbor played a pivotal role in the Pacific within a few short months of the Japanese attack.

U.S. Navy crewmen watch as a B-25 Mitchell bomber takes off from the USS *Hornet* for the initial air raid on Tokyo, called the Doolittle Raid, in April 1942. The Doolittle Raid was planned to improve American and Allied morale and to inflict damage on the morale of the Japanese.

That Pearl Harbor and the American fleet rebounded so quickly has led many historians to conclude that the Japanese attack was ultimately a failure. Certainly, the future of the Combined Fleet proved to be bleak. Of the six aircraft carriers that sailed under Nagumo on December 7, not a single one survived the war. The *Akagi*, *Kaga*, *Soryu*, and *Hiryu* were all sunk at the Battle of Midway in June 1942. Damaged severely at the Battle of the Coral Sea, the *Shokaku* met its end in 1944, when it was sunk near the Marianas Islands. The *Zuikaku* went to the bottom of the sea in October 1944 during the Battle of Leyte Gulf in the Philippines. In addition to the six aircraft carriers that launched the raid against Pearl Harbor, every other ship and submarine in the First Carrier Striking Force was reported either sunk or missing at sea by the time Japan surrendered in September 1945. Minoru Genda and Mitsuo Fuchida lived to see the destruction of the fleet they helped build and lead and the end of the war it started. Admirals Yamamoto and Nagumo did not. Yamamoto was killed in April 1943, when his plane was shot down by American fighters near the Solomon Islands. Having failed to bring final victory to Japan, Nagumo committed suicide in 1944.

The aftermath of the Pearl Harbor attack was no less dramatic for Japanese and Japanese-American citizens. The people of Japan celebrated their warriors, who, it seemed early on, had struck a mortal blow against the empire's greatest military, political, and racial foe. For decades, the Japanese had suffered the indignity of being considered racially inferior by what Yamamoto once labeled an "arrogant enemy [who] made light of us."[6] The victory in Hawaii erased that stain and returned to the Japanese a measure of respect that they felt Imperial Japan deserved. The defeat of the Pacific Fleet, combined with simultaneous victories over the British in Asia, represented a triumph over the white Westerners who had always disparaged Asians in general, the Japanese in particular. Yet as the war years passed, it became clear to the Japanese people that they would pay a terrible price for their single moment of glory. By 1945, Japan's cities lay in ruins, utterly demolished by massive American fire-bomb raids and two atomic attacks. After four disastrous years of war, the same men and women who had applauded the returning sailors and airmen of the First Carrier Striking Force found themselves starving, homeless, and defeated. For many Americans at the time, the imagined treachery of the attack on Pearl Harbor justified the utter obliteration of Japan and its military establishment. Few people in the United States mourned as American bombers leveled cities such as Tokyo,

Hiroshima, and Nagasaki. Japan's population experienced the destruction of their society and the deaths of countless loved ones, at home and on the battlefields of the Pacific, in return for victory on December 7.

More than 100,000 Americans of Japanese descent also suffered for Japanese military success on a single morning. Even before the attack, some of the Japanese officers who knew about the attack suspected that their compatriots in the United States would answer for it. As Nagumo's task force approached Hawaiian waters, for example, a rear admiral overheard a conversation in the wardroom of his ship in which an officer commented, "What an awful experience it will be for the Japanese residents of Hawaii after our air raid there."[7] The admiral was troubled by these words because his own "older brother was living in Honolulu." "What kind of retaliation will he receive," he wondered.[8] The admiral's concern, while understandable, was misplaced. With such a large Asian, and specifically Japanese, population, Hawaii would prove more or less immune to the paranoia and racial hatred that quickly infected the western United States. As rumors spread of a possible Japanese invasion of the West Coast, a move far beyond the capabilities of a Japanese military that at any rate was focused on the southwestern Pacific, latent racism generated an anti-Japanese backlash. Japanese-American businesses were boycotted, and Japanese-Americans who had lived in the United States for generations were harassed on the streets and taunted with racial insults. White households turned their backs on Japanese families that lived next door. Japanese schoolchildren were teased and bullied by boys and girls who had been their friends just days before. Even Chinese Americans mistaken for Japanese were subjected to harassment.

Popular fear and anger found official political expression in Executive Order 9066. Consumed by the prospect of a followup attack on the Western states, the federal government took action against the region's 117,000 Japanese people, immigrants and citizens alike. The authorities imagined the Japanese community to be a potential nest of spies and saboteurs who would prepare the way for a Japanese invasion. Almost to the last, of course, these "suspects" were either law-abiding residents or loyal patriotic citizens. A handful of Japanese agents were indeed operating in the United States, but there is no credible evidence that the Japanese community as a whole presented a threat to national security. Still, the mere presence of men, women, and children who looked like and shared a heritage with the enemy made many in the West, and in Washington, D.C., nervous. As early as January 1942, West Coast politicians were clamoring for federal action to place "all Japanese, whether citizens or not . . . in inland concentration camps."[9] Accordingly, on February 19, 1942, President Roosevelt signed Executive Order 9066, which gave Lieutenant General John L. DeWitt, head of the Western Defense Command, the authority to "relocate" Japanese people who lived in the Western states to internment camps.

The presidential order was quickly enforced, and, through-out the West, Japanese civilians were rounded up and sent to 10 relocation centers set up far from the coast. The order was intended to confine Japanese Americans there for the dura-tion of the war. Nothing could effect their release. The fact that 33,000 young Japanese-American men enlisted in the U.S. armed forces meant little. Their families remained in the camps even as the men who belonged to the Japanese-American 442nd Regimental Combat Team won 18,143 decorations for valor while fighting the Germans in France and Italy. When Japanese Americans sought legal relief from their woes, they were rejected at all levels, including the Supreme Court. In four cases that involved Japanese-American citizens who refused to adhere in one way or another to the restrictions placed on them by Executive Order 9066, the court ruled that they had violated the law and were not protected under the U.S. Constitution. Guilty of nothing more than being of Japanese descent, these American citizens could be rightfully counted among the casu-alties of Pearl Harbor.

While Japanese Americans were enduring the hardships of living with the fear and racism of their fellow citizens and

their own government, Admiral Husband E. Kimmel and
Lieutenant General Walter Short were being subjected to the
scrutiny of a shocked and humiliated nation. Investigations
into exactly what happened at Pearl Harbor began within
weeks of the attack. Between December 1941 and May 1946,
10 separate sets of hearings were convened by either Congress
or the Navy. Each examined, in detail, the events that led up to
the attack, focusing on the conduct of the officers in command
of the U.S. forces at Pearl Harbor. Both Kimmel and Short had
been relieved of duty on December 17, 1941; the next day, the
first hearing was called. The two men subsequently spent the
next five years defending their decisions and conduct during

EXECUTIVE ORDER 9066

One of the most regrettable episodes in American history began in
February 1942. Bowing to paranoia heightened by latent racism,
President Roosevelt vented the nation's anger and frustration by
authorizing the internment of Japanese-American citizens. Internment
of civilian foreign nationals is common during wartime: German and
Italian civilians were assigned to special camps after both of those
countries declared war on the United States in December 1941.
The difference in the Japanese-American case lay in the fact that
the internees were U.S. citizens, fully deserving of the protections
against seizure of persons and property without due process guaranteed by law and the United States Constitution. They received neither
and paid a price for Pearl Harbor that was asked of no other groups
of citizens simply because of their ethnic origins. Portions of the
text of the internment authorization, Executive Order 9066, are
offered here.

the lead-up to the attack. Neither ever accepted full responsibility for the disaster that unfolded on their watch. Kimmel and Short repeatedly claimed that they had done the best they could, given the resources and intelligence available to them. One hearing after another, however, found the men, to greater or lesser degrees, guilty of serious lapses in judgment and poor command decisions. Having been placed on inactive duty in 1942, both officers retired in protest and continued their defense as civilians. Walter Short, reduced in rank to major general, pleaded his case vigorously until his death in 1949. Husband Kimmel, similarly reduced to rear admiral, did likewise during the years before his death in 1968.

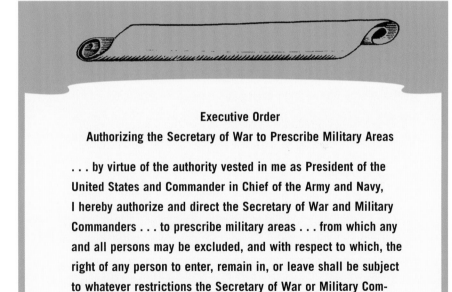

Executive Order
Authorizing the Secretary of War to Prescribe Military Areas

. . . by virtue of the authority vested in me as President of the United States and Commander in Chief of the Army and Navy, I hereby authorize and direct the Secretary of War and Military Commanders . . . to prescribe military areas . . . from which any and all persons may be excluded, and with respect to which, the right of any person to enter, remain in, or leave shall be subject to whatever restrictions the Secretary of War or Military Commanders may impose in his discretion. . . . The Secretary of War is hereby authorized to provide for residents of any such area who are excluded therefrom, such transportation, food, shelter, and other accommodations as may be necessary. . . .*

---

* Henry Steele Commager, *Documents of American History, Volume II* (New York: Apple-Century-Crofts, Inc., 1958), p. 645

The aftermath of Pearl Harbor touched the United States in myriad ways. Indeed, to one extent or another, this single two-hour air raid altered American history and reshaped the contours of World War II while affecting the lives of both ordinary people and political leaders. The world on December 8 was a far different place in terms of how people conceived of themselves, their nation, and their collective future. A memory, a legacy, had been created that lived on longer and more powerfully than anyone in 1941 could have imagined. The recall-

9/11 AND PEARL HARBOR COMPARED

One of the first Americans to compare Pearl Harbor and the terrorist attacks of 9/11 was President George W. Bush. Yet President Bush went one step further than most people when he explicitly tied the memory of Pearl Harbor not only to the destruction of the World Trade Center but also to the war in Iraq. For the president, as the excerpt below from a December 7, 2005, speech before the Council on Foreign Relations demonstrates clearly, Iraq was merely the latest battlefield on which Americans combated the forces of tyranny. Thus he could make a direct connection between Pearl Harbor and the current conflict between democracy and global terrorism.

> Today we mark the anniversary of a fateful day in American history. On December 7, 1941, our peaceful nation awoke to an attack plotted in secret, and executed without mercy. The strike on Pearl Harbor was the start of a long war for America—a massive struggle against those who attacked us, and those who shared their destructive ambitions. Fortunately for all of us, a great generation of Americans was more than equal to the challenge. Our nation pulled together—and despite setbacks and

ing and retelling of the events of December 7, in other words, established a set of criteria by which Americans interpreted the past and present. Every American president since then, for example, has worried about a surprise attack on American soil by a vicious enemy. This fear helped build the American military machine that opposed the Soviet Union during the Cold War (1945–1990). Pearl Harbor convinced average Americans that their enemies could and would attack without warning. The nuclear first-strike policy of the United States government

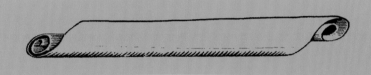

battlefield defeats, we did not waver in freedom's cause. With courage and determination, we won a war on two fronts: we liberated millions, we aided the rise of democracy in Europe and Asia, we watched enemies become allies, and we laid the foundation of peace for generations. On September 11th, 2001, our nation awoke to another sudden attack. In the space of just 102 minutes, more Americans were killed than we lost at Pearl Harbor. Like generations before us, we accepted new responsibilities, and we confronted new dangers with firm resolve. Like generations before us, we're taking the fight to those who attacked us . . . and like generations before us, we will prevail . . . this war will take many turns, and the enemy must be defeated on every battlefront. . . . Yet the terrorists have made it clear that Iraq is the central front in their war against humanity. So we must recognize Iraq as the central front in the war on terror.*

*"President Discusses War on Terror and Rebuilding Iraq." Available online. URL: www.whitehouse.gov/news/releases/2005/12/20051207-1. html, August 18, 2007.

President Franklin D. Roosevelt signs the declaration of war following the Japanese bombing of Pearl Harbor at the White House on December 8, 1941, while several members of Congress look on.

was intended to demonstrate the American resolve not to be taken unawares again. When President John F. Kennedy, himself a veteran of World War II, was told that the Russians had placed medium-range nuclear missiles on the island of Cuba, only 90 miles from the United States, he responded by citing the example of Pearl Harbor. If the Russians refused to remove the weapons, he was ready to attack Cuba before they became operational. According to the president's brother, Attorney General Robert F. Kennedy, such aggressiveness guaranteed that there would be no "Pearl Harbor type attack"[10] on the president's watch.

The fear that a surprise attack could be launched against the United States at any moment eased somewhat with the end of the Cold War. It flared once more, however, suddenly and intensely, on September 11, 2001. Almost as soon as terrorists had slammed two jetliners into the World Trade Center in New York City, the comparisons with Pearl Harbor began. Once again, it seemed to most Americans, an enemy had caught the United States off guard despite years of warnings. Terrorists had already tried unsuccessfully to blow up the World Trade Center in 1993, and the American destroyer USS *Cole* had been targeted by suicide bombers on a boat seven years later. American embassies in Africa had been bombed in 1998, and Osama bin Laden, the leader of al Qaeda, had openly announced his intention to attack Americans at home. That his organization was planning an attack was well known to American intelligence agencies. Still, despite all the warning signs, the 9/11 bombers got through, just like the Japanese bombers had gotten through in 1941. President George W. Bush felt the comparison between 2001 and 1941 to be so apt that he supposedly wrote in his diary on September 11, the "Pearl Harbor of the 21st century took place today."[11] The explosions at Pearl Harbor echoed through the streets of New York City on 9/11. Notwithstanding the many and obvious differences between the Japanese raid and the terrorist bombing, Americans used the idea of Pearl Harbor to create a context for understanding the second deadliest attack on American soil in the nation's history.

The damage wrought by the First Carrier Striking Force on December 7, 1941, was repaired quickly, and the United States Navy went on to help win the war in the Pacific. What survived much longer was the notion that Americans are always subject to surprise attacks because of their lack of preparedness. This idea, in a sense, became Pearl Harbor. Much more so than ships and planes, historic battles, and even World War II itself, the imagined day of December 7 and the imagined place called Pearl Harbor have endured to shape and reshape how the United States sees itself and its place in the modern world.

CHRONOLOGY

1853   Commodore Matthew Perry arrives in Japan.

1894–1895   Sino-Japanese War is fought, giving Japan its first opportunity to control China.

1898   Spanish-American War is fought in the Philippines.

1904–1905   Russia and Japan go to war; U.S. president Theodore Roosevelt negotiates the peace.

1907   United States drafts War Plan Orange, a plan for war with Japan.

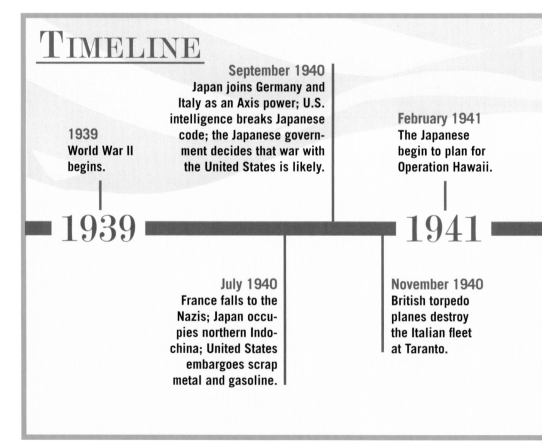

TIMELINE

September 1940
Japan joins Germany and Italy as an Axis power; U.S. intelligence breaks Japanese code; the Japanese government decides that war with the United States is likely.

1939
World War II begins.

February 1941
The Japanese begin to plan for Operation Hawaii.

1939

1941

July 1940
France falls to the Nazis; Japan occupies northern Indochina; United States embargoes scrap metal and gasoline.

November 1940
British torpedo planes destroy the Italian fleet at Taranto.

1909   Japanese strategists begin to prepare for war with the United States.

1914–1918   World War I is fought in Europe and Asia.

1919   Treaty of Versailles is signed, ending World War I.

1921–1922   Washington Naval Disarmament Conference meets to set global levels of warships.

1924   United States begins code breaking work against Japan; the Mitchell Report predicts an attack on Pearl Harbor if a war with Japan breaks out.

1928   Simulated air raids against Pearl Harbor are carried out by the aircraft carrier USS *Langley*; Yamamoto

April 1941
Chief of Naval Operations Admiral Stark warns Pearl Harbor about possible Japanese surprise attack on a weekend; Martin-Bellinger Report predicts a Japanese attack on Pearl Harbor at dawn by carrier-based planes.

July 1941
Japan occupies southern Indochina; United States embargoes oil and freezes Japanese assets in America.

November 1941
The First Carrier Striking Force assembles at Hitokappu Bay and sails for Hawaii.

1941   1941

September 1941
The Japanese government orders the military to prepare for war with America; U.S. intelligence intercepts message from Tokyo to Hawaii asking for details on depth of Pearl Harbor and ships located there.

December 1941
Pearl Harbor is attacked by Japanese air and naval forces.

proposes attack against enemy fleet using air-dropped torpedoes.

1929   Great Depression begins.

1931   The Japanese invade Manchuria.

1936   Japanese army officers try to overthrow the government; subsequent changes put admirals and generals in the Japanese government.

1937   Japan invades China; Japan signs Anti-Comintern Pact.

1938   Simulated air raids against Pearl Harbor are carried out by the aircraft carrier USS *Saratoga*.

1939   World War II begins.

1940   France falls to the Nazis (July); Japan joins the Rome-Berlin Axis (September); American MAGIC system breaks the Japanese diplomatic code (September); the British bomb the Italian fleet at Taranto (November).

1941   The Japanese bomb Pearl Harbor; United States enters World War II.

1945   World War II comes to an end.

NOTES

CHAPTER 1

1. Henry Berry, *"This is No Drill!"—Living Memories of the Attack on Pearl Harbor.* New York: Berkley Books, 1992, p. 75.
2. Ibid., p. 165.
3. Ibid., p. 161.
4. Ibid.
5. Gordon Prange, Donald M. Goldstein, and Katherine V. Dillon, *God's Samurai: Lead Pilot at Pearl Harbor.* Washington, D.C.: Brassey's, 1990, p. 35.
6. Berry, *No Drill*, p. 161.
7. Donald M. Goldstein and Katherine V. Dillon, eds., *The Pearl Harbor Papers: Inside the Japanese Plans.* Dulles, Va.: Brassey's, 2000, p. 250.
8. Henry Steele Commager, ed., *Documents of American History, Volume II.* New York: Apple-Century-Crofts, 1958, p. 631.

CHAPTER 2

1. Jeffrey P. Mass, ed., *Court and Bakufu in Japan: Essays in Kamakura History.* Stanford, California: Stanford University Press, 1982, p. 124.
2. Merion Harries and Susie Harries, *Soldiers of the Sun: The Rise and Fall of the Imperial Japanese Army.* New York: Random House, 1991, p. 10.
3. Alan Trachtenberg, *The Incorporation of America: Culture and Society in the Gilded Age.* New York: Hill and Wang, 1982, p. 15.
4. Ibid., p. 67.

5. Jerald A. Combs, *The History of American Foreign Policy.* New York: Alfred A. Knopf, 1986, p. 163.
6. Henry Steele Commager, ed., *Documents of American History, Volume II*, p. 225.

CHAPTER 3

1. Prange, Goldstein, and Dillon, *God's Samurai*, p. 7.
2. Combs, *American Foreign Policy*, p. 260.
3. Thomas G. Paterson, *Major Problems in American Foreign Policy, Volume Two: Since 1914.* New York: D.C. Heath Company, 1989, p. 175.
4. Ibid.
5. Berry, *No Drill*, p. 153.
6. Paterson, *Major Problems*, p. 175.
7. Ibid., p. 177.
8. Gordon Prange, Donald M. Goldstein, and Katherine V. Dillon, *Pearl Harbor: The Verdict of History.* New York: McGraw Hill Book Company, 1986, p. 68.

CHAPTER 4

1. John W. Lambert and Norman Polmar, *Defenseless: Command Failure at Pearl Harbor.* St. Paul, Minn.: MBI, 2003, p. 59.
2. Ibid., p. 24.
3. Donald M. Goldstein and Katherine V. Dillon, *The Pearl Harbor Papers: Inside the Japanese Plans.* Washington, D.C.: Brassey's, 1993, pp. 116–117.

4. B.H. Liddell Hart, *History of the Second World War.* New York: G.P. Putnam's Sons, 1970, p. 210.

5. Goldstein and Dillon, *Pearl Harbor Papers*, p. 13.

6. Ibid., p. 26.

7. Ibid., p. 37.

8. Lambert and Polmar, *Defenseless*, p. 59.

9. John W. Dower, *War Without Mercy: Race and Power in the Pacific War.* New York: Pantheon Books, 1986, p. 103.

10. Ibid.

11. Ibid., p. 109.

12. Ibid.

13. Paterson, *Major Problems*, p. 215.

14. Prange, *Pearl Harbor*, p. 30.

15. Ibid., p. 32.

16. Ibid., p. 4.

17. Ibid., p. 117.

18. Harries, *Soldiers of the Sun*, p. 292.

CHAPTER 5

1. Harries, *Soldiers of the Sun*, p. 292.

2. Lambert and Polmar, *Defenseless*, p. 134.

3. Goldstein and Dillon, *Pearl Harbor Papers*, p. 59.

4. Ibid., p. 27.

5. Ibid., p. 29.

6. Ibid.

7. Combs, *American Foreign Policy*, p. 286.

8. Goldstein and Dillon, *Pearl Harbor Papers*, p. 16.

9. Ibid., p. 30.

10. Ibid., p. 114.

11. Prange, *Pearl Harbor*, p. 312.

12. Ibid.

13. Ibid., p. 100.

14. Goldstein and Dillon, *Pearl Harbor Papers*, p. 151.

15. Akira Iriye, *Pearl Harbor and the Coming of the Pacific War: A Brief History with Documents and Essays.* Boston: Bedford/St. Martin's, 1999, p. 76.

16. Prange, *Pearl Harbor*, p. 652.

17. Ibid.

CHAPTER 6

1. Iriye, *Pearl Harbor and the Coming of the Pacific War*, p. 87.

2. Ibid., p. 82.

3. Ibid.

4. Goldstein and Dillon, *Pearl Harbor Papers*, p. 38.

5. Lambert and Polmar, *Defenseless*, p. 79–80.

6. Goldstein and Dillon, *Pearl Harbor Papers*, p. 224.

7. Berry, *No Drill*, p. 166.

8. Iriye, *Pearl Harbor and the Coming of the Pacific War*, p. 97.

9. H.P. Willmott, *Pearl Harbor.* London: Cassell, 2001, p. 95.

10. Prange, *God's Samurai*, p. 33.

CHAPTER 7

1. Lambert and Polmar, *Defenseless*, p. 90.

2. Ibid.

3. Wilmott, *Pearl Harbor*, p. 101.

4. Ibid.

5. Goldstein and Dillon, *Pearl Harbor Papers*, p. 43.

6. Ibid., p. 79.

7. Ibid., p. 89–90.

8. Ibid., p. 160–161.

9. Wilmott, *Pearl Harbor*, p. 124.

10. Lambert and Polmar, *Defenseless*, p. 92.

11. Ibid.

12. Berry, *No Drill*, p. 39.

13. Ibid.
14. Iriye, *Pearl Harbor and the Coming of the Pacific War*, p. 104.
15. Ibid., p. 105.
16. Berry, *No Drill*, p. 165.
17. Ibid., p. 69.
18. Prange, P*earl Harbor*, p. 5.

CHAPTER 8

1. Berry, *No Drill*, p. 28.
2. Goldstein and Dillon, *Pearl Harbor Papers*, p. 194.
3. Ibid., p. 227.
4. Berry, *No Drill*, p. 166.
5. Paterson, Major, *Problems in American Foreign Policy, Volume Two*, p. 189.
6. Goldstein and Dillon, *Pearl Harbor Papers*, pp. 121, 122.
7. Ibid., p. 186.
8. Ibid., p. 195.
9. Peter Irons, *Justice at War: The Story of the Japanese American Internment Cases*. Berkeley: University of California Press, 1983, p. 7.
10. Paterson, *Major Problems*, p. 558.
11. David Williard, "Pearl Harbor and 9/11: Stuck in a Recurring Narrative." Available online. URL: www.wm.edu/news/?id=2708, accessed August 18, 2007.

BIBLIOGRAPHY

Berry, Henry. *"This is No Drill!"—Living Memories of the Attack on Pearl Harbor*. New York: Berkley Books, 1992.

Combs, Jerald A. *The History of American Foreign Policy*. New York: Alfred A. Knopf, 1986.

Commager, Henry Steele, ed. *Documents of American History, Volume II*. New York: Apple-Century-Crofts, Inc., 1958.

Dower, John W. *War Without Mercy: Race and Power in the Pacific War*. New York: Pantheon Books, 1986.

Goldstein, Donald M., and Katherine V. Dillon, eds. *The Pearl Harbor Papers: Inside the Japanese Plans*. Dulles, Va.: Brassey's, 2000.

Harries, Merion, and Susie Harries. *Soldiers of the Sun: The Rise and Fall of the Imperial Japanese Army*. New York: Random House, 1991.

Iriye, Akira. *Pearl Harbor and the Coming of the Pacific War: A Brief History with Documents and Essays*. Boston: Bedford/ St. Martin's, 1999.

Irons, Peter. *Justice at War: The Story of the Japanese American Internment Cases*. Berkeley: University of California Press, 1983.

Lambert, John W., and Norman Polmar. *Defenseless: Command Failure at Pearl Harbor*. St. Paul, Minn.: MBI, 2003.

Liddell Hart, B.H. *History of the Second World War*. New York: G.P. Putnam's Sons, 1970.

Paterson, Thomas G. *Major Problems in American Foreign Policy, Volume Two: Since 1914*. New York: D.C. Heath Company, 1989.

Prange, Gordon, Donald M. Goldstein, and Katherine V. Dillon. *God's Samurai: Lead Pilot at Pearl Harbor.* Washington, D.C.: Brassey's Inc., 1990.

Trachtenberg, Alan. *The Incorporation of America: Culture and Society in the Gilded Age.* New York: Hill and Wang, 1982.

Williard, David. "Pearl Harbor and 9/11: Stuck in a Recurring Narrative." College of William and Mary. Available online. URL: www.wm.edu/news/?id=2708, August 18, 2007.

Willmott, H.P. *Pearl Harbor.* London: Cassell, 2001.

Further Reading

Anderson, Charles Robert. *Day of Lightning, Years of Scorn: Walter C. Short and the Attack on Pearl Harbor.* Annapolis, Md.: Naval Institute Press, 2005.

Borch, Frederic L. *Kimmel, Short, and Pearl Harbor: The Final Report Revealed.* Annapolis, Md.: Naval Institute Press, 2005.

Carlisle, Rodney P., ed. *One Day in History—December 7, 1941.* New York: Collins, 2006.

Madsen, Daniel. *Resurrection: Salvaging the Battle Fleet at Pearl Harbor.* Annapolis, Md.: Naval Institute Press, 2003.

Mazer, Henry. *A Boy at War: A Novel of Pearl Harbor.* New York: Simon and Schuster Books for Young Readers, 2001.

Odo, Franklin. *No Sword to Bury: Japanese Americans in Hawai'i During World War II.* Philadelphia: Temple University Press, 2004.

Richardson, Kent D. *Reflections on Pearl Harbor: An Oral History of December 7, 1941.* Westport, Conn.: Praeger Publishers, 2005.

WEB SITES

Pearl Harbor Raid, December 7, 1941

www.history.navy.mil/photos/events/wwii-pac/pearlhbr/pearlhbr.htm

National Geographic: Remembering Pearl Harbor

plasma.nationalgeographic.com/pearlharbor/

"December 7, 1941–Japanese Bomb Pearl Harbor," The History Place

www.historyplace.com/worldwar2/timeline/pearl.htm

Photo Credits

INDEX

ABOUT THE AUTHOR

JOHN C. DAVENPORT holds a Ph.D. from the University of Connecticut and currently teaches at Corte Madera School in Portola Valley, California. Davenport is the author of several biographies, including that of the Muslim leader Saladin, and has written extensively on the role of borders in American history. He lives in San Carlos, California, with his wife, Jennifer, and his two sons, William and Andrew.